IMAGES
of Aviation

LUNKEN AIRFIELD

The iconic Art Deco terminal centers Lunken Airport in this view from the late 1960s. Bounded by the Little Miami River, with residential homes and a Cincinnati water treatment plant for neighbors, Lunken has thrived over the last century despite its location. With the Cincinnati Aviation Heritage Society headquartered there, Lunken is a repository of regional aeronautical history as well as a busy commercial airport. (Cincinnati Aviation Heritage Society.)

ON THE COVER: Members of the fledgling Embry-Riddle Company pose in front of their Waco 10 biplane at Lunken in 1927. Pictured are, from left to right, John Paul Riddle, Richard Blythe, Talton Higbee Embry, Charlie Myers, and John Woods. The complete photograph is on page 19. (Embry-Riddle Aeronautical University.)

IMAGES
of Aviation

LUNKEN AIRFIELD

Stephan Johnson and Cheryl Bauer

ARCADIA
PUBLISHING

Published by Arcadia Publishing
Charleston, South Carolina

Library of Congress Control Number: 2011939993

For all general information, please contact Arcadia Publishing:
Telephone 843-853-2070
Fax 843-853-0044
E-mail sales@arcadiapublishing.com
For customer service and orders:
Toll-Free 1-888-313-2665

Visit us on the Internet at www.arcadiapublishing.com

Dedicated to Bob Johnson and Randy McNutt, who never let us down

CONTENTS

ACKNOWLEDGMENTS

The Cincinnati Aviation Heritage Society (CAHS), the Hans Dam Collection at Wright State University (HDC, WSU), and Embry-Riddle Aeronautical University (ERAU) are the primary sources for this book. Charlie Pyles of CAHS was instrumental in gathering, scanning, and identifying many photographs. The Lunken family was also most helpful. Our appreciation also goes to John Anderson of WSU, who organized the extraordinary images and ephemera collected by Mr. Dam, and to Kevin Montgomery of ERAU for sharing rare early photographs and providing Stephen G. Craft's account of Embry-Riddle's early days at Lunken.

Don Bedwell's research and writings on Lunken and American Airlines were invaluable. Mike O'Bryant searched out many newspaper accounts of events at Lunken over the years. The staff of the Public Library of Cincinnati and Hamilton County and the staff of the Photograph Division of the Library of Congress were also helpful.

Jack Klumpe, veteran photographer for the *Cincinnati Post*, and Kevin Grace and Suzanne Maggard of the University of Cincinnati were integral in securing several photographs. We also appreciate the help and materials provided by Fred Anderton, Lunken Airport manager; Michael Banks; Steven Beasley; Silvana Dimitrova; Don Fairbanks; Lindsey Hamilton of the Cincinnati branch of ERAU; Greg Morehead; Edward Przybyla of the Tristate Warbird Museum; Hal Shevers; Dick Swaim; and Sarah Rickman.

Written sources referred to include "Lunken Airport" by Don Bedwell (*Timeline*, Oct.-Dec. 2006), *Silverbird: The American Airlines Story* by Don Bedwell (Sandpoint, ID: Airways International Inc., 1999), *National Air and Space Museum* by C.D.B. Bryan (New York: Harry N. Abrams, 1979), *Barnstorming* by Martin Caidin (New York: Duell, Sloan and Pearce, 1965), *Once Around the Patch of Life: The Autobiography of Don Fairbanks*, edited by Eugenia Christensen (author-published), *I Could Never Be So Lucky Again* by Gen. James H. Doolittle, with Carroll V. Glines (John P. Doolittle Family Trust, 1991), *Official AAF Guide Book* (New York: Pocket Books, 1944), *Barnstormers and Speed Kings* by Paul O'Neil (New York: Time-Life Books, 1981), and *Out of the Blue and Into History* by Betty Stagg Turner (Arlington Height, IL: Aviation Publishing, 2001).

INTRODUCTION

Lunken Airfield was where Cincinnatians began to embrace flying in the 1920s. On Sunday afternoons, they drove their Model As and Pontiacs to Wilmer Road at the city's eastern edge to marvel at the barnstormers and daredevils who seemed to fear nothing. Thomas G. Foxworth captured their attitude in *The Speed Seekers* when he wrote, "Long before any flying regulations had been framed, when no one was watching except incredulous landlubbers, these carefree knights of the air skimmed between trees and over barntops . . . drinking in the exhilaration like some heady wine."

Lunken crowds ate French-Bauer ice cream and downed soda pop as they pondered soaring in a Curtiss Jenny biplane assembled from a World War I surplus kit. As they welcomed aviation legends, including Charles Lindbergh and Amelia Earhart, some dreamed of flying aeroplanes and of racing them for big money and fame.

Underlying the excitement and spectacle of early aviation was the sobering reality of how dangerous it truly was. These pioneers were bursting through clouds and soaring across oceans in aircrafts that were basically flying gas tanks equipped with bare-bones instruments. Many people featured in this book died in aerial accidents.

Lunken Airfield focuses on Lunken from inception through its glory days as the nation's largest municipal airport. Geography is often destiny, and Lunken, bordered by the Little Miami and Ohio Rivers, has always been affected by its location. Benjamin Stites established the Columbia settlement there in 1788. Beleaguered by flooding, settlers sought higher ground, leaving the area to wild turkeys that spawned the name Turkey Bottoms. Later, Cincinnati Polo Club members practiced there and farmers raised corn.

Biplanes replaced polo ponies at Turkey Bottoms as World War I fueled interest in aviation. People were intrigued by how aircraft could defend the country as well as transport people and products more efficiently. The world was changing in unimaginable ways, and Ohioans, thrilled with the Wright brothers' accomplishments, were determined to be part of the future.

Barnstormers lured the public with their aerobatics and cheap rides. Hugh Watson and John Dixon "Dixie" Davis were among the first. Davis, who trained with the Royal Canadian Air Force during World War I, is said to have started giving flying lessons at Turkey Bottoms in 1921. In 1922, Watson, a former Army flight instructor, and Robert Wheat operated two commercial aircraft from Watson's four-acre field in Madeira, according to Karl F. Burckhardt's 1930 account. In 1923, Watson moved to Grisard Field in Blue Ash, where the Reserve Corps of the 100th Division Army Air Service had established itself in 1922. Other pilots also used the area, including John Paul Riddle, a Kentucky native who had flown in the Air Service.

Industrialist Eshelby F. Lunken, a partner in the Grisard Company, met wealthy investor Talton Higbee Embry at Blue Ash. Riddle taught Embry to fly. Embry and Lunken had the money; all three believed that aviation would drive the century. They left Grisard for Turkey Bottoms in search of land for expansion and better access to other city transportation. Former Grisard president John Sage and secretary John W. Pattison, one of Watson's early students, joined Lunken with his father, Edmund H. Lunken, to form the Lunken Airport Company (LAC).

LAC, with 126 stockholders, developed 218 acres that the Lunkens had purchased. Nicholas Longworth, a longtime US Congressman, donated 11 adjacent acres. By 1924, the site was being called Lunken Airport. Army major E.L. Hoffman moved the reserve squadron hangars from Grisard to Lunken. Davis and Wendell Pavey established the short-lived Dixie Davis Flying Field nearby in 1925. Watson moved his operations to Lunken for one year but then returned to Blue Ash to establish Watson Airport.

Soon Embry and Riddle formed an aviation company, leasing facilities at Lunken. They offered aerial photography, transport services, and flight lessons and sold Waco, Fairchild, and Velie aircraft. In 1925, they opened the Embry-Riddle Flying School, which became one of the first five flight schools that were nationally approved by the US Department of Commerce. It was one of only two institutions that were approved as transport, limited commercial, and private flying schools.

Charles Lindbergh's visit to Lunken in August 1927 stoked public enthusiasm. Lindbergh had made the first solo transatlantic flight in May, and was on a goodwill tour to 75 cities. Crowds thronged his motorcade, which formed at the main hangar, from the airfield to Redland Ball Park. As Lindbergh addressed the Redlands crowd, answered journalists' questions at the Sinton Hotel, and spoke to a crowd of 1,200 at an elegant banquet at the Gibson Hotel, he reiterated that aviation was the future of American commerce, travel, and military. The first step, he said, was to build adequate public airports.

At that time, city and LAC officials were already discussing developing Lunken as a municipal airport. Lindbergh's visit provided momentum. Cincinnati voters approved a $500,000 bond issue that fall to expand and upgrade the airfield into a municipal airport. The Lunkens signed a perpetual lease to the city, and the council accepted the airfield in 1928. The city then purchased an additional 870 acres, while preparing to build three hangars and install better lighting and navigational aides for night flying.

The Embry-Riddle Company (E-R) became Cincinnati's first regular airmail carrier when it received US Post Office Airmail Contract 24 in November 1927. The daily flight from Cincinnati to Chicago via Indianapolis made the "Queen City" one of a handful in the nation to have direct airmail service. Although planes had improved since 1918, when the first airmail pilots were referred to as the "Suicide Club," flying the mail was still hazardous. Because the pilots had to fly in the very worst kinds of weather, and often over dangerous terrain lacking landmarks, their life expectancy was only two years. Between May 1918 and February 1921, 26 airmail personnel died, wrote Barry Rosenberg and Catherine Macaulay in *Mavericks of the Sky*.

Embry-Riddle pilots fared better, but there was no guarantee that they would make it safely to their destination. While testing a proposed commercial route between Louisville and Cleveland in May 1927, E-R pilots set a record for forced landings, according to Stephen G. Craft. In a four-hour period, they had to land seven times, either because they were lost due to lack of landmarks or because of extreme fog. The company boasted that there were no injuries or fatalities among its airmail pilots in 1928, but it appears pilots were overworked. Pilot Frank Merrill flew 11,682 miles that July, when bus drivers and train engineers were only allowed to travel 4,500 miles in a month. Nevertheless, the airmail route brought recognition to E-R and to Lunken Airport. Passengers began flying on mail flights in February 1928.

Thomas E. Halpin, who formed the Metal Aircraft Corporation, began building the single-engine Flamingo at the airfield in 1928. One of the first all-metal planes built in America, the plane could carry 2,050 pounds, and it cost $19,325. Its dependability and enclosed cabins enabled E-R to become a passenger airline service.

A crisis within E-R in 1928 began a chain of events that figured in the creation of American Airlines. To keep its airmail contract, E-R had to acquire larger planes to carry the burgeoning amount of mail. The Fairchild Aircraft Company offered to help buy new planes—and to purchase E-R as a subsidiary—until its own holding company, Aviation Corporation, bought a large share of E-R and other air carriers that delivered mail.

The merger between E-R and the Aviation Corporation (AVCO) allowed E-R to expand service to western states but cost the company its flight school in 1930. That same year, AVCO created a new subsidiary—American Airways. In 1932, E-R moved its headquarters and most of its employees to St. Louis to merge with American Airways. In 1934, American Airways became American Airlines and was a major carrier at Lunken for years.

In 1929, five businessmen incorporated the Aeronautical Corporation of America, later Aeronca, to build a light aircraft for personal and recreational use. The company is generally recognized as the first manufacturer of a commercially successful light aircraft, according to aviation historian Don Bedwell.

Other flying services that began in the late 1920s were hurt by the Depression. Mason & Dixon Air Lines provided service between Cincinnati and Detroit for a few months before being bought by Marquette Airlines in 1931. The Main Flying Service, which flew between Cincinnati and Pittsburgh, also lasted only a few months.

Although the Depression deepened, Lunken's development gave Cincinnatians hope. Visits by more celebrity pilots stirred the public's excitement about flying. Women flyers were particularly intriguing. By mid-1929, only 31 of the more than 4,500 licensed pilots in the United States were women. Several pilots, including Amelia Earhart, stopped at Lunken following the first Women's Air Derby in 1929. Earhart and her contemporaries countered the patronizing attitudes they often face with daring comments and hands-on demonstrations of their skills. She told the *Cincinnati Enquirer* on August 26, 1929, that the main lesson she learned from the derby was that "the girls and women handle their ships just as competently as the male aviators."

That fall, she and three other derby competitors formed the Ninety-Nines, a group dedicated to improving opportunities for women pilots. Named for the number of charter members, the organization became international with thousands of members over the years. Most of the women featured here are, or were, members of the Ninety-Nines, including Gladys O'Donnell. In 1930, she won the Women's Air Derby and $6,250—several years' wages for the average worker then. O'Donnell also made a splash in the Cincinnati papers when she won the western division of the Cord Cup race in 1932. Cord Cup pilots praised Lunken's runways and field layout, and a Cincinnati spokesman expressed hope that their positive reports would spread nationwide. In the same way, the women hoped a good report on one would lead to greater acceptance of all women flyers.

In September 1930, more than 25,000 people attended a three-day dedication of Lunken as Cincinnati's municipal airport. Thousands more watched the aerial action from the hills of Cincinnati and northern Kentucky. The Lunken crowd listened to jazz by Paul Whiteman's orchestra and heard officials speak, but the real attractions were the stunt flyers and the racers competing in an air derby sponsored by Henry Ford. Lt. Jimmy Doolittle, who had performed the first public blind landing without instruments in 1929 and was famous for his aerobatics, was the headliner. Howard Hughes, the 25-year-old aircraft manufacturer, pilot, and movie producer, sponsored a *Hell's Angels* aerobatic contest, named for his World War I flying epic. He and his new discovery, Jean Harlow, handed out the trophies at Lunken on September 27 and September 28 respectively.

In addition to the glamour of daredevils and movie stars, Cincinnatians embraced aviation in very practical ways. By 1936, 200 young men were studying aviation at the Automotive High School (AHS), a branch of Cincinnati Public Schools, in Mount Auburn. Started during World War I to address the urgent need for automotive training, the school offered its first aeronautics course in 1929. Five years later, students were reconditioning planes and building new aircraft, often testing them at the airfield. Many Lunken employees were AHS graduates.

By 1936, greater Cincinnati had six airports: Lunken, Crosley Airport in Sharonville, Western Hills Airport, Watson Airport, Hugh Watson Field, and Mount Healthy Airport. Lunken was the biggest. Due to the size of its concrete runways, Lunken was the largest commercial airport in the United States by 1930. At that time, Lunken had two concrete runways measuring 4,028 feet. Only three other airports in the world, located in Berlin, London, and Paris, were larger, Burkhardt wrote.

Work began in 1936 on a new terminal featuring nine ticket counters and a luxurious restaurant, the Sky Chef. Construction was completed by January 1937, when disaster struck. A record-setting flood swamped over 12 square miles of Greater Cincinnati. The surging Little Miami River shut down flights at Lunken for 17 days and ultimately changed the airport's future. Dedication of the new terminal was postponed until May 1938. More than 75,000 people attended. Despite growing concerns about Lunken's viability to become an international airport, expansion continued.

In 1939, Mary Hinsch and her brother Charles A. Hinsch Jr. funded the airport's first radio-operated control tower in honor of their father, Charles A. Hinsch Sr., who had been president of Fifth Third Bank as well as an early—and persuasive—advocate for aviation in Cincinnati. The control tower drew Transcontinental & Western Airlines (T&WA) and Delta Airlines to Lunken by 1941. Delta flights provided a needed commercial link to the South with direct flights to Atlanta. Marquette Airlines provided service to five midwestern cities.

During World War II, Lunken averaged 11,000 operations monthly, according to research by Stuart L. Faber, a founding member of the Cincinnati Aviation Heritage Society. At the onset of the war, Frank Mayo Fairchild, Lunken's first control tower operator, developed an important air traffic control course for prospective military aviation cadets and students of the Civilian Pilot Training Program. The Army Air Corps' Air Transport Command, which provided worldwide air service for troops and cargo, quietly operated out of Cincinnati as well.

On August 15, 1942, the public thrilled to a demonstration of the Army's new Vultee Vengeance bomber by Lt. John West at Lunken. "Camouflaged in war colors, the bomber hurtled across the field in a roaring blur, pulled up suddenly into a steep climb, made a snap roll, then streaked earthward with lightning fury, leveling off just 25 feet above the ground," recounted the Works Progress Administration guidebook.

Women flyers were also active. Jacqueline Cochran, whose husband controlled Consolidated Vultee Aircraft, visited Cincinnati in 1940 to advocate using women pilots to free male commercial pilots for military duties. She later headed recruiting and training for the Women's Flying Training Detachment (WFTD). Meanwhile, Nancy Harkness Love founded the Women's Auxiliary Ferrying Squadron (WAFS) to ferry military planes to wherever they were needed for training or prepping for deployment.

By June 1943, Cincinnati was headquarters for the WAFS's Ferrying Division with Love in charge. The WFTD and WAFS merged into the Women Airforce Service Pilots (WASP) in August 1943. Cochran led the WASP, with Nancy Love still running the Ferrying Division out of Cincinnati. Her husband, Col. Robert M. Love, flew into Lunken when he was reassigned to Cincinnati in 1944. The airport doubtlessly saw many other wartime partings and reunions.

After the war, Cincinnati officials began to look for a new airport site to accommodate more flights and provide international service. Despite the rerouting of the Little Miami River following the 1937 flood, Lunken's low elevation and frequent fog were still concerns. While options were being considered, northern Kentucky officials made an offer that the major airlines couldn't refuse. In 1947, American Airlines, Delta, and TWA (formerly T&WA) moved their operations to the new Greater Cincinnati and Northern Kentucky International Airport (CVG) near Covington, Kentucky.

Nevertheless, "Lunken survived that exodus to become one of the nation's busiest general aviation airports by the mid-1950s," Bedwell wrote in 2006. Edmund P. Lunken, son of Eshelby Lunken, started Midwest Airways at the airport in 1963, offering scheduled flights to Columbus, Cleveland, Detroit, and Chicago. Chartered weekend jaunts in the summer were made to Michigan in Midwest's small fleet of Lockheed Electra 10As. Midwest closed in 1967, and Lunken sold the Electras. But the airport continued as a reliever for CVG while serving as a hub for commuter airlines, private pilots, celebrities, and corporate planes. Notably, Proctor & Gamble established its corporate hangar there.

Higbee Embry and Paul Riddle's legacy is Embry-Riddle Aeronautical University, which has over 150 campuses worldwide. The Cincinnati branch, located in Sharonville, had approximately 200 students actively pursuing degrees in aviation programs, technical management, and project management in 2011.

In 2011, CAHS was applying to the National Register of Historic Places to have the entire airport designated as a historic district. Yet even while embracing its history, Lunken keeps moving forward. In 2011, the airport had more than 70 charter and commercial flights daily to national and international destinations, and the public continued to enjoy air shows there.

One

THOSE AMAZING FLYING MACHINES

Early aviation photographs often have a pastoral feel to them because that's where pilots landed—in fields. This group poses with Hugh Watson's Curtiss Jenny at Turkey Bottoms around 1924. Watson is in the center of the photograph with his hand on his hip, wearing goggles and helmet. To the immediate right of him John Paul Riddle. Riddle and Watson taught scores of people to fly and helped popularize aviation in Greater Cincinnati. (HDC.)

Embry-Riddle began regular airmail service from Lunken in the 1920s, but plans for airmail service started much earlier. Paul Peck, shown above, flew the first US Post Office–sanctioned airmail exhibition as part of the Queen City Aviation Meet at Coney Island from July 19 to July 21, 1912. He flew 560 postcards and letters from the park to the village of California nearby. The post office was trying to demonstrate that the public could entrust its mail to pilots for more rapid delivery. Like many early aviation events, the proceedings were as much about entertaining the public as making flying history. Coney's roller coaster tracks are visible to the right, below. Called a "gypsy" stunt pilot by a reporter, Peck died in Chicago on September 12, 1912, when his plane spun in while stunting. (Both, HDC.)

Aviatrix Ruth Law's determination is obvious as she gazes from a Wright Model B biplane in July 1915 in Cincinnati. The aviation pioneer devised a unique map-reading device to keep her route constantly in view for a record-setting nonstop 590-mile flight between Chicago and Hornell, New York, in 1916. It was a national distance record for men and women and an international record for women. (HDC.)

In 1917, Law returned to Cincinnati to give a demonstration at the Sharonville Speedway. Here, she prepares to land her Curtiss Pusher on the speedway as spectators watch, amazed. Flying was still very much a novelty, and a woman pilot was an absolute rarity. Pres. Woodrow Wilson honored her at a 1916 dinner. The Army Air Service rejected her when she volunteered in 1917 to fly in World War I. (HDC.)

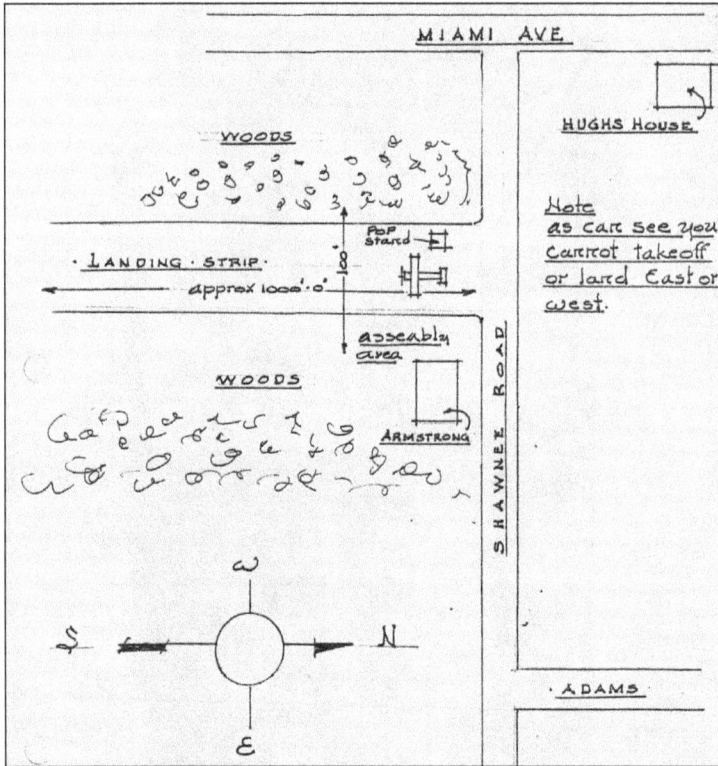

MIAMI AVE.

WOODS

HUGHS HOUSE.

Note
as can see you
cannot takeoff
or land East or
west.

· LANDING · STRIP ·
approx 1000'.0'

Pop
stand

assembly
area

WOODS

SHAWNEE ROAD

ARMSTRONG

W

S ————— N

E

· ADAMS ·

In 1922, Maj. Hugh Watson, a World War I veteran, shared a house with his brother Parks on the north side of Shawnee Road in Madeira and operated an airfield across the street. Watson and Robert "Zack" Wheat's two planes were the "first commercial planes operated in Cincinnati," wrote Karl F. Burckhardt in 1930. People crowded onto the field on Sunday afternoons to watch stunting and sometimes cadge a ride. (HDC.)

1st J.b. IN MADERIA.

Hugh Watson (wearing goggles) prepares to take off at his Madeira Airfield in 1922. Wheat left the business after a few months and sold his plane to inventor Powel Crosley Jr. These pioneers flew almost by instinct. "An instrument panel . . . would only confuse them," wrote a contemporary. In the time-honored male tradition, Wheat was nicknamed for Brooklyn Robins (later Dodgers) outfielder Zack Wheat, whose nickname was "Buck." (HDC.)

14

Passengers embark on the Cincinnati riverfront from a Curtiss flying boat in 1920 while a crowd gathers. Taking a plane ride was still a novelty—and something of a challenge—at the time. Almost any type of flying event drew a good crowd, although most folks could only afford to watch. On this day, the Ohio Valley Aero Transport Company was charging $50 for a 15-minute ride. (HDC.)

Charles Edwin Lay stands between two flyers with a Curtiss Jenny around 1921 at Turkey Bottoms. His son, John T. Lay, is on the right with his hand on the wing. Charles was a barnstormer who started Cincinnati Aircraft Company in 1920 and had a flying field for a time in the Madisonville area. John served in the Navy in the Pacific in World War II and later operated cinemas around Cincinnati. (HDC.)

Knickers, ties, leather helmets, and goggles were part of the pioneer flyers' wardrobes. Members of the early E-R Company at Lunken around 1925 are, from left to right, T. Higbee Embry, John Paul Riddle, Richard Blythe, and Stanley C. "Jiggs" Huffman. Riddle grew up in Pikeville, Kentucky, served in the US Army Air Service, and then became a barnstormer. One day in 1921, he landed at Turkey Bottoms in the middle of a polo match. "They all chased me with mallets," Riddle said in a January 11, 1956, *Cincinnati Post* article. "Then they got interested in the airplane and I made $400 taking polo players up for rides." Embry, a wealthy Cincinnatian, went to Riddle to learn to fly. After seven days of instruction, Embry soloed in a Waco 9. The men became good friends and soon went into business with Hugh Watson at Grisard Field. Believing that the new airport planned for Turkey Bottoms would be the better location for future expansion, Embry and Riddle started an aviation company there. Embry-Riddle Aeronautical University is the legacy of that early partnership. (HDC.)

Two

AN AIRFIELD IS BORN

Pioneer parachutist Paul DeWeese (left), John Dixon "Dixie" Davis (center), and Hugh Watson stand with Watson's Curtiss biplane around 1926. Davis, a World War I veteran and stunt pilot, started giving rides for 2¢ per pound along with flying lessons at Turkey Bottoms around 1924, which drew attention to the area's potential as an airfield. Wendell Pavey, his business partner, died in a plane crash near Coney Island in 1925, and Davis's business ventures seemed jinxed. In September 1930, just days before Lunken's dedication, Davis died during an air circus at Muncie, Indiana, when his plane's right wing collapsed as he was performing a stunt. (HDC.)

Four generations of Lunkens pose on May 17, 1942. Edmund Pattison (E.P.) Lunken holds his son, Edmund Backus (E.B.). Next to him is his father, Eshelby F., and grandfather, Edmund H. Lunken. Edmund H. and Eshelby, with their business partners, signed over the airfield to the Cincinnati council. The Lunkens, whose original name was Lunkenheimer, made their fortune manufacturing valves, a business they sold in 1962. (Lunken Family Collection, CAHS.)

The official opening of Lunken as a commercial airfield in 1924 saw a group of investors and employees gather around the aptly named *Big Boy* biplane that belonged to the Johnson Flying Service. The Lunken Airport Company wooed the US Army Air Service into moving its hangars from Grisard Field to Wilmer Avenue. The new company also built a runway and converted a horse barn into a machine shop. (HDC.)

Members of the fledgling E-R Company promoted aviation with "missionary zeal," wrote Stephen G. Craft in a company history. "If it's flying we do it. If it's airplanes we have them," was the company's slogan. Company cofounders pose around 1927 in front of a Waco 10 made by the Advance Aircraft Company of Troy, Ohio. In addition to the Wright brothers' triumphs, Ohioans were eager to be part of building and flying the ships that would take Americans to the future. Embry-Riddle was determined to be a part of that adventure. The partners officially formed the company on December 17, 1925, with T. Higbee Embry as president and John Paul Riddle as general manager. They began with one hangar that already existed and then built an office building, Craft wrote. Pictured are, from left to right, John Paul Riddle, Richard Blythe, T. Higbee Embry, Charlie Myers, John Woods, and Harry Sherwin. (ERAU.)

Other members of the early E-R team included, from left to right, Warren R. Vine (maintenance manager), Jiggs Huffman (engineering officer), T. Higbee Embry, John Paul Riddle, Fred Davis (operations manager), and Albert Wunder (business manager). E-R soon became a regional distributor for Waco, Fairchild, and Monocoupe airplanes, although business was so slow initially than Embry bought the first plane, and his mother, Susan, bought the second. She became the company vice president. (ERAU.)

E-R's first office building saw an influx of business as the 1920s progressed. The company offered flight training, charter and cargo service, aerial photography, and eventually air mail service. It was an enthusiastic aviation promoter and constantly worked on ways to sell the idea of aviation to the public, including contests for school children, a radio program, and dropping copies of its magazine from a plane onto lawns and barnyards. (ERAU.)

Instructors prepare to begin a flying lesson with a Waco 10 around 1927. This photograph is from Joseph Field, who was a pioneer in aviation instruction with the E-R Flight School. A competitive racer, Field placed fifth in the Trans-Continental Air Races in 1932. (ERAU.)

Ralph E. Meguire stands in front of an Embry-Riddle flying school plane around 1927. The original caption reads, "just sworn in." Meguire may have just been sworn into the Army Air Corps Reserve, which maintained facilities at Lunken. At the age of 20, he became the youngest pilot in the Embry-Riddle division of American Airways, copiloting the Cincinnati-to-Atlanta run. (ERAU.)

EMBRY·RIDDLE COMPANY

FIVE OF THE EMBRY-RIDDLE TRANSPORT PILOTS

A COMPLETE AIR SERVICE

EMBRY-RIDDLE operates the fastest and most luxurious transportation system between the gateway to the south, Cincinnati —through Indianapolis, the capital of Indiana and Chicago the center of big business for the middle west. The company also has available the most modern flying equipment for charter to any destination, any time. Rates furnished upon application.

The Embry-Riddle Flying School is one of three in the United States to be inspected and approved by the Department of Commerce, Washington, D. C. All courses from private pilot to finished transport with night flying experience, are offered.

A complete sales and service department is maintained with adequate facilities for repair and overhaul. The company acts as distributor for the following manufacturing concerns, Fairchild, Waco, Mono-Aircraft, Flamingo, Gliders, Inc., and Wright Aeronautical Corporation.

The Photographic Department is completely equipped for any type of aerial views or mapping.

General Offices of the Company
LUNKEN AIRPORT - CINCINNATI, O.
Telephone East 4700

EXTERIOR OF ONE OF THE PASSENGER PLANES

SEATING COMPARTMENT

CONTROLS AND DASH BOARD

USE AIR MAIL

This c. 1929 brochure shows E-R pilots in uniforms, which was a major change from jodhpurs and leather jackets. The Flamingo shown has a basic instrument panel and wicker or rattan seats, favored for their light weight. E-R stressed professionalism in every service it offered. The brochure notes that the flight school is only one of three nationally certified by the Aeronautics Branch of the US Department of Commerce as approved flight schools. Many instructors were World War I veterans, including Robert L. Rockwell, who ran the school in 1928. In 1916, he flew with the Lafayette Escadrille, a volunteer group of Americans fighting for the French before America entered the war. After American Airways absorbed E-R's Lunken business, Paul Riddle moved to Florida. There, E-R trained 25,000 World War II pilots, and during the Korean War, it trained Air Force mechanics. Following the Vietnam War, E-R consolidated its training programs into a college, which was accredited as Embry-Riddle Aeronautical University (ERAU) in the late 1960s. As of 2011, ERAU has two main campuses, located in Florida and Arizona, plus 150 branch campuses throughout the world. (CAHS.)

By the time this photograph was taken in 1930, Monocoupes were used in the E-R flying school. World War I veteran Ike Vermilya, who ran the school at the time, began an intensive 30-lesson ground school course that was approved by the Aeronautics Branch of the US Department of Commerce. The class could be taken at Lunken or as an extension course. (Morris Hall Collection, CAHS.)

Harold Mathny, an E-R employee, demonstrates how to don a parachute in 1929. Parachute jumping was added to the flight school curriculum in 1927. At first, an expert parachutist from Wright Field near Dayton came to Lunken to instruct students. By 1928, students went to Wright Field for parachute instruction and to study the effects of wind turbulence on aircraft. (ERAU.)

Paul Riddle, shown above to the right, flew Powel Crosley Jr.'s Waco 10 in the 1927 National Air Tour. Below, the plane, named the *Crosley Stork*, is shown after landing at the Detroit Airport. Crosley (left) was a wildly successful entrepreneur and inventor who became an investor in Thomas E. Halpin's Flamingo airplane, which was built at Lunken. National air tours, also called reliability tours, were held to promote aviation and to demonstrate airplanes' reliability. In 1928, Embry paid $1,000 to bring the Ford Reliability Good Will Tour to Lunken. Tours also featured stunt pilots like James H. "Jimmy" Doolittle to entertain the crowds. (Above, CAHS; below, ERAU.)

Pilot Paul Riddle, his wife, Grace, and Harry Sherwin deliver the Crosley Corporation's patented new Bandbox radio to two unidentified sales representatives in Grand Rapids, Michigan, during the 1927 National Air Tour. Crosley, whose future holdings included WLW radio and the Cincinnati Reds, was interested in promoting and capitalizing on new technology, new means of communication, and new forms of transportation. He had purchased his first plane from Hugh Watson's partner back in the Madeira airfield days and continued to be involved in aviation. He eventually started his own airport in Sharonville and built some aircraft, including the *Crosley Flea*. Radio and air travel had grown from being alien concepts at the start of the 20th century to being the embodiment of technological advancement by the 1920s. Manufacturers of a little red wagon for youngsters chose to call their product the RadioFlyer, combining the most exciting technologies of the time to stir the imaginations of children. (ERAU.)

Above, an E-R employee loads mail onto a Waco JTO Taperwing on a snow-covered field in 1928. The mail route flew from Cincinnati to Indianapolis to Chicago. In November 1927, the company received the contract from the US Post Office to carry the mail for $1.47 per pound. Two pilots were assigned to make the daily flights, but if the need arose, Embry and Riddle also flew the mail. Issuing postcards with mail pilots' photographs (below) was another way the company promoted airmail service. School children were asked to create an airmail slogan. One of the three winners was "To Speed It There, Use the Air." The promotions worked. In July 1928, when bus drivers and locomotive engineers were restricted to 4,500 travel miles monthly, Frank Merrill (below) flew 11,682 miles on 21 round trips. (Both, ERAU.)

Ford Tri-Motors, such as the one pictured above, were revered by pilots for their reliability and durability in the late 1920s and the 1930s. They were the first all-metal transport planes. Richard E. Byrd thought so highly of them that he made the first flight over the South Pole in one. E-R invested in them to fly its extended mail and passenger service to Indianapolis and Chicago. (ERAU.)

Waco biplanes line up on the E-R flight line at Lunken in 1929. Although public demand for personal planes was very slow initially, by the end of 1926, E-R's Waco sales totaled $30,000. Weaver Aircraft Company of Lorain, Ohio, first built Wacos in the early 1920s. After the firm folded, Waco production was taken over by Advance Aircraft Company of Troy, Ohio, which started in 1925. At a time when small aircraft makers proliferated, Advance became known as one of the most innovative, reliable manufacturers. Waco launched its Model 9 in the 1925 National Ford Air Tour. The Model 10, an improved, streamlined version, appeared in 1927. Flyers were soon won over by the Waco 10 because of its smooth handling, durability, and easy maintenance. The plane won a class in the 1927 Air Derby, creating even more demand for the model. Advance had produced 1,900 Wacos by 1929, selling them in the United States and overseas. The company, the leader in its field, renamed itself Waco Aircraft that same year. (ERAU.)

Catherine Boyers tries out an Aeronca C-2 at Lunken around 1929. Catherine and her husband, Albert, were co-owners of the first airport in northern Kentucky, located in Ross. Women flyers were still rare; of the 4,500 licensed flyers in June 1929, only 31 were women. But those women who took up flying invariably fell in love with it. Several women attended the Embry-Riddle Flight School. (CAHS.)

Pilot Louise Thaden steps out of the cockpit of her Travel Air J-5 shortly after winning the first Women's Air derby in 1929. At the time of the race, the Arkansas native held the women's records for altitude, speed, and endurance. Whenever she saw an airplane, her credo was "I want to fly it, I can fly it, and I will fly it." (CAHS.)

Howard Hughes had just released *Hell's Angels* when he sponsored an acrobatic competition of the same name at Lunken's dedication as a municipal airport in 1930. The spins, barrel rolls, loops, and chandelles provided "some of the best entertainment" of the three-day event, reported the September 29 *Enquirer*. Unlike the making of the movie, where two stunt pilots and one mechanic died, the competition went smoothly. (Library of Congress.)

HOWARD HUGHES' Thrilling Multi-Million Dollar -Air Spectacle

HELL'S ANGELS

JEAN HARLOW
Ben Lyon
James Hall

Hughes brought Jean Harlow, the platinum blonde of his World War I epic, to Lunken to present prizes to the acrobatics winners. The starlet presented the first-place cup to Stanley "Jiggs" Huffman of E-R and the second-place prize to Thomas Halpin, the Flamingo maker. Meanwhile, *Hell's Angels*— the most expensive movie ever made at the time—was being shown at the Shubert Theater in Cincinnati. (CAHS.)

Famed stunt pilot Jimmy Doolittle thrilled crowds with 300-mile-per-hour bursts across Lunken Field, "outside loops, upside down flying, barrel rolls, Immelmanns and whatnot," according to the *Cincinnati Post* on September 27, 1930. A headliner wherever he appeared, Doolittle participated in many Lunken air shows and races. He made the first transcontinental flight across the US in one day in 1922, covering 2,163 miles. (Library of Congress.)

Over 25,000 people visited the $1.2-million airport during the dedication. What had 15 years earlier sheltered corn farmers, duck hunters, and polo players was now the largest airport in the United States and the largest landing surface in the world, Karl F. Burckhardt wrote in 1930. The Lunkens and their investors, city officials, and voters who approved a $500,000 bond issue in 1927 made it happen. (CAHS.)

Three

THE FLIGHT BUSINESS TAKES OFF

From the beginning, planners intended Lunken to be much more than just an airport. It was to be the center for all things related to flying. The Cincinnati City Council offered facilities at low rents to encourage businesses and manufacturers. Thomas E. Halpin started the Metal Aircraft Corporation there in 1928 to produce a metal-skinned monoplane he named the Flamingo. Here, two men look over a new Flamingo inside Halpin's factory around 1929. (CAHS.)

An early pilot recalled making his first flights in planes made of canvas and bailing wire. Here, Morris Hall of Embry-Riddle stitches fabric at Lunken in 1929. Fabric portions of the planes were treated with a concoction referred to as "dope" that tightened and waterproofed the fabric around the framework. (Morris Hall Collection, CAHS.)

Socialite Pauline Longworth christens a Flamingo plane for Mason & Dixon Air Lines at Lunken on July 20, 1929. Her father, US Congressman Nicholas Longworth, had donated land when the airfield was originally being configured. (CAHS.)

A Flamingo G-2 in the E-R fleet prepares to take off around 1930. The metal monoplane was the first original aircraft built in Cincinnati. Although the plane's designer, Thomas Halpin, came from the prestigious Stout Aircraft Company and had Powel Crosley Jr. as a key investor, the Flamingo did not outlive the Depression. Only 21 Flamingos were built, and only one is known to exist today, in South America. (CAHS.)

Mason & Dixon Air Lines passengers flew in these Flamingos between Cincinnati and Detroit for a $15 fare in the late 1920s. Flamingos are remembered because of adventurer Jimmie Angel's flight in one in 1937. Angel landed one atop a high waterfall in Venezuela. Lacking space to take off, he had to abandon the plane. Today, the cataract is named Angel Falls, and the Flamingo is on display in Ciudad Bolivar, Venezuela. (HDC.)

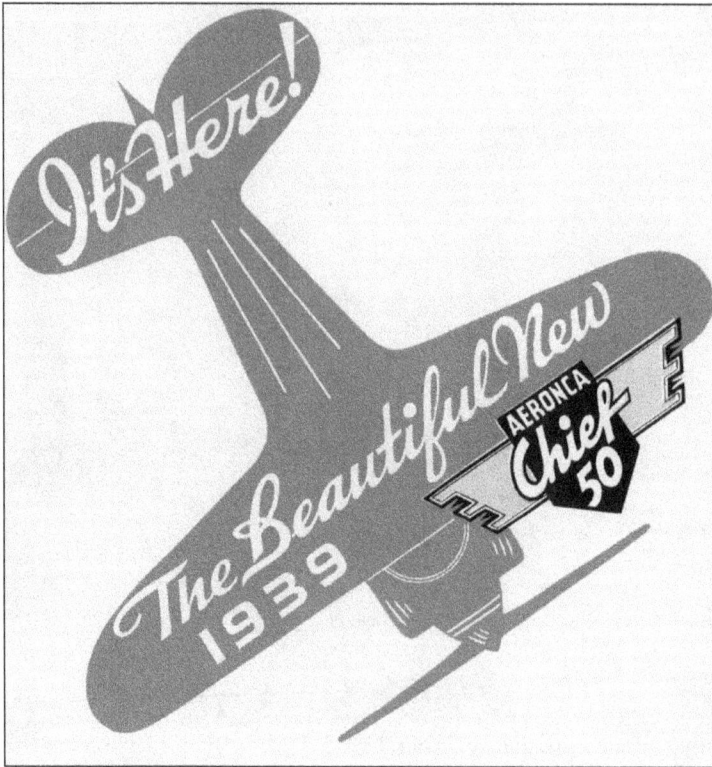

The National Air and Space Museum recognizes Aeronca as the first manufacturer of a commercially successful light aircraft. The 1939 Aeronca Chief 50 featured air and oil ("oleo") shock absorbers in the landing gear and side-by-side seating. The Chief line boosted horsepower from 42 horsepower to 50, keeping Aeronca competitive with a growing number of aircraft manufacturers. The ultimate Super Chief, built in 1940 after Aeronca left Lunken, had 65 horsepower. (HDC.)

An Aeronca C-3, designed by the firm's chief engineer Roger Schlemmer, sits in front of the Hangar 4 factory in 1934. The two-seater C-3 sold for $1,800, with an optional left-hand door available for an additional $15. The two-cylinder, air-cooled engine used three gallons of fuel and a pint of oil per hour. A round trip from Lunken to Miami, Florida, then took 46 hours and required 15 stops. (HDC.)

A prototype for the Aeronca K awaits a test flight by Bob Koster in January 1937. Roger Schlemmer created the design for a safer stunt plane. After the 1937 flood ruined the factory, Aeronca moved to Middletown, Ohio. The company, under various owners, built small military aircraft that were used extensively in World War II and, later, personal planes until late 1951. Aeronca then switched to building parts for other aircraft. (HDC.)

One of the earliest planes to be flown and sold at Lunken was the Velie Monocoupe. Willard L. Velie, a former automaker, joined with aircraft designer Don Luscombe to produce the first Monocoupes in 1928 in Moline, Illinois. An immediate success, a new version with improved landing gear debuted in 1929. Around 1929, E-R used the plane to fly mail, and earlier, it used them to transport passengers. (ERAU.)

Embry-Riddle used this Waco 10, as well as a Fairchild FC-2, to deliver mail in 1929. Two days before the first mail flight, all five E-R craft had been sidelined due to various problems. Another Waco was purchased at the last minute. As dignitaries gathered to mark the maiden flight, a sign painter was still lettering the US mail contract number on the Waco. (Morris Hall Collection, CAHS.)

A mechanic readies a Stout Airlines Ford Tri-Motor while two passengers talk during a stop at Lunken around 1927. William Stout's company provided the first regularly scheduled passenger service in the US. In 1926, Stout employed the first flight steward, who worked on the Detroit–to–Grand Rapids flight. There were no stewardesses until 1930. (CAHS.)

Designed especially for the sportsman . . . the 1934 Waco Cabin

The Ultimate in Airplane Design

IS

the 1934 Waco Cabin

Cruising speed — 130 m.p.h.   Top speed — 150 m.p.h.

Slow Landing   Quick Take-off

Demonstrations at Any Time

CHARTER TRIPS   INSTRUCTION

AERIAL ADVERTISING and PHOTOGRAPHY

STORAGE and SERVICE

U. S. Government Approved Repair Station No. 124

QUEEN CITY FLYING SERVICE, Inc.

Authorized Waco Distributors

LUNKEN AIRPORT   Hangar No. 1   CINCINNATI, OHIO

Telephone: EAst 4630

Queen City Flying Service published this advertisement for the 1934 Waco cabin model in hopes of drumming up some Depression-era business. The popular Wacos did manage to continue selling through the lean years. Lawrence Maxwell "Max" Schmidlapp and George J. "Pappy" Wedekind ran Queen City at the time. William S. Roseler, the original company president, died in a tragic accident in 1933. At the time, Roseler was a 30-year-old Woodlawn resident and graduate of the Embry-Riddle Flight School. He was substituting one night for a stunt pilot who didn't show up for a job at Coney Island. Roseler was giving an aerial exhibition involving fireworks when something went wrong. Horrified spectators saw Roseler's plane suddenly nose down. He jumped, but his parachute failed to open and he died from the fall. Schmidlapp and Wedekind ran the successful business for decades until Edmund P. Lunken and Bud Hilberg took over in the early 1960s. (HDC.)

A mechanic checks out the engine on a Pitcairn Super Interstate at Lunken on December 7, 1930. The large landing light on the right wing enabled the plane to fly the night mail. Lunken had runway lights by 1926, closely following Cleveland Municipal Airport, which had lighted runways by 1925. Aviation entrepreneur Harold Pitcairn later contributed to the further development of the practical helicopter. (CAHS.)

A Stinson SB-1 Detroiter of the E-R fleet stands ready to fly mail and passengers between the Queen City, Indianapolis, and Chicago. In 1928, the company transported 270 passengers, 2,014 pounds of cargo, and 35,667 pounds of mail. One method to promote airmail was a Talking Air Mail Box in Fountain Square, where an unseen person talked and joked with people mailing letters or just passing by. (ERAU.)

A Pan American Airways plane stops at Lunken for refueling in 1928. The Ford Tri-Motor plane ran on a new Pratt & Whitney Wasp engine of 425 horsepower that was much more powerful than the earlier Wright J-4 engine of 200 horsepower or the Wright 975-1 engine of 300 horsepower. The Wasp was used on many aircraft types because of its power and reliability. (CAHS.)

This Wright-Bellanca 2 Columbia, seen at Lunken in 1929, was the plane that Charles Lindbergh wanted to use on the first Atlantic crossing. Lindbergh ended up flying a Ryan M-1 monoplane. The W-B 2 (one of only three built) is seen here without the pontoon that could be mounted between the wheels. (Morris Hall Collection, CAHS.)

The *City of Jackson* readies for takeoff at Lunken in 1929. The plane may have belonged to Pioneer Airways from the logo on the back of one man's coveralls. A $500,000 bond issue passed in the fall of 1927 generated improvements that made Lunken the largest public airport in the country. (CAHS.)

By 1930, American Airways (AA) had acquired Embry-Riddle and was operating out of Hangar 1. This Curtiss-Wright T-32 Condor at Lunken was the last of the US biplane airliners, according to American Airlines historian Don Bedwell. The aerodynamic features of the plane are at odds with the dated upper wing. This plane was destroyed in a hangar fire on September 27, 1932, at Floyd Bennett Field in New York. (CAHS.)

American Airways was renamed American Airlines in 1934, the same year that the company became the first to offer sleeper plane service on transcontinental flights. AA introduced stewardesses who served cold fried chicken dinners on the Condor biplane in 1933. Management wanted to convince the public that air travel could be just as comfortable and safe as traveling by train. This 1934 advertisement compares the sleeping berths to trains' sleeping compartments, and notes that there is no extra charge for the accommodations. AA continued to entice customers with assurances that the airline had the most experienced pilots, with "half a million to a million and a half flying miles per man," and the most capable stewardesses, who were "schooled in meal service and in dietetics, capable nurses to aid with children, courteous, helpful, ready with the little comforts," according to a 1937 advertisement. (CAHS.)

The Vultee V-1A was the fastest in AA's fleet in 1934. Due to its small size and single engine, government regulators limited it to daylight flights, so AA retired the plane from passenger service in 1936. The all-metal plane, built by the Airplane Development Corporation, carried eight passengers. (CAHS.)

By the early 1930s, Embry-Riddle's original facility in Hangar 1 bore the American Airlines name and logo. Retired General Electric engineer Art Leonard of Indian Hill learned to fly in an Aeronca C-3 similar to the one shown here and graduated to B-52s in the Air Force. As a student pilot in Kansas, Leonard learned how to compensate for the C-3's tendency to ground loop when landing in crosswinds. (CAHS.)

Nelson Ronsheim photographed AA's *Flagship Arkansas* on October 7, 1939. The Flagship line started with the use of Douglas DC-3s, promising the most luxurious amenities for passengers and a smoother ride. AA executives had gone to the Douglas Aircraft Company with a list of requirements for a new plane: it must be able to sleep 14 passengers, carry more during day flights, have more powerful engines, and the have a redesigned tail to improve stability. A 1940 advertisement for the Flagship flights shows a man shaving with an electric razor that was provided by the airline, a woman writing a letter, and other passengers enjoying gourmet meals and comfortable sleeping berths. When the sleek aircraft was first introduced in 1936, some observers thought they were so futuristic that they looked like props for a science fiction movie, wrote AA historian Don Bedwell. (Nelson Ronsheim photograph, Copyright 2012, Michael G Smith.)

A mechanic signals to the pilot of this Transcontinental and Western Airlines (T&WA) DC-3, photographed by Nelson Ronsheim in January 1941. Both T&WA, which became Trans World Airlines after 1946, and Delta began flights at Lunken that year. The US Army Air Corps commandeered the plane for service in 1942 and 1943. Bolivia's president used it in the 1950s. (Nelson Ronsheim photograph, Copyright 2012, Michael G Smith.)

Businessmen prepare to board a Lockheed 10A Electra operated by Midwest Airways in 1963. Edmund P. Lunken started Midwest that year to reinstate scheduled commercial passenger service at the airport. The line provided service to Columbus, Cleveland, Detroit, and Chicago, as well as summer weekend jaunts to Michigan for about four years, according to E.B. Lunken, Edmund's son. (Lunken Family Collection, CAHS.)

Four

YOU SAW WHO
AT HANGAR TWO?

Among the many flyers who stopped to service their planes at Lunken in the 1920s and 1930s were a number of famous pilots and movie stars. The airport's accessible location and increasing size made it a natural stop. Charles Lindbergh, a good friend of Paul Riddle, visited unofficially many times. Here, Lindbergh watches as his Curtiss is serviced on April 28, 1928. Lindbergh is the only man without a hat. Among the onlookers is Riddle, to Lindbergh's left, wearing helmet and goggles. Just one month earlier, the *Enquirer* had reported on a Lindbergh visit, when he "spoke warmly of the future of air mail and . . . the aircraft industry." This candid snapshot is from Elmer Schmidt's album. Schmidt and his brother Melville operated the Cincinnati Aircraft Service at Hangar 2 for many years. (HDC.)

Roscoe Turner flashes a devil-may-care grin before his LTR-14 Meteor. Striking in a light blue British-cut uniform, Turner visited Lunken often. He was the only three-time winner of the Thompson Trophy Race, a 100-mile test of speed and racing skill. In 1930, Turner set a transcontinental airspeed record of 12 hours and 33 minutes, beating Frank Hawks's previous record. In 1933, he won the prestigious Bendix Transcontinental Race. (HDC.)

Turner sold sundries from his Sikorsky *United Cigar Store* on Lunken visits around 1926. The Sikorsky was reconfigured to resemble a German Gotha bomber for Howard Hughes's epic *Hell's Angels*. While filming a scene in 1927 in which the bomber catches fire, the stunt pilot heard a wing spar snap. He parachuted in time, but Phil Jones, the mechanic intent on simulating the fire, died in the ensuing crash. (CAHS.)

Turner greets local racing enthusiasts around 1935. Always a popular draw at air shows and races, Turner was also a stunt pilot during the making of *Hell's Angels*. The Corinth, Mississippi, native sometimes flew with Gilmore, a pet lion cub that was named for his sponsor, the Gilmore Oil Company. Gilmore started flying at five weeks and had a special cub-sized parachute. He was grounded when he became a full-size lion and moved to a Los Angeles habitat. In 1934, Turner placed second in the transport category of the London-to-Melbourne MacRobertson International Air Derby. He traveled 11,300 miles in 92 hours, 55 minutes, and 30 seconds in a Boeing 247D aircraft. By 1942, he was also a proven acrobatic pilot. During a demonstration at Lunken of the Army's new Vultee Vengeance dive-bomber that August, Turner, a consummate showman, delighted thousands of spectators as he pivoted a 20-year-old Ford Tri-Motor above the field. His flight school trained about 3,000 pilots during World War II. He later started Turner Airlines in Indianapolis and was an honorary official at the Indianapolis 500. (CAHS.)

Frank Monroe Hawks (right) shakes hands with T. Higbee Embry in June 1929. Hawks instructed prospective flying cadets during World War I. In 1919, he gave an impressionable Amelia Earhart her first plane ride. Hawks set over 200 flying records, including two transcontinental air speed records in 1929. Lunken crowds knew him as a gregarious racer and stunt pilot with a gleaming Douglas Fairbanks smile. He flew a "cloud buster," a Model R Travel Air Mystery Ship, seen below at Lunken in 1930. It was a swift, high-performance, low-wing monoplane that outflew the Army's biplane fighters. It was referred to as a mystery ship because the first three Model Rs were built in secrecy, and it sharpened public anticipation to see them. (Above, CAHS; below, Morris Hall Collection.)

Ruth Elder, a movie actress and pilot, wanted to duplicate Lindbergh's feat. In October 1927, at age 23, she and copilot George Haldeman attempted to fly nonstop across the Atlantic in her Stinson Detroiter, named *American Girl*. Precautions for the rough-weather flight included following charted shipping lanes and carrying inflatable rubber suits. Three hundred miles short of Paris, they ditched in the Atlantic due to an oil leak. A Dutch tanker rescued them, but the plane caught fire and was destroyed. Nevertheless, New York City threw Elder and Haldeman a ticker tape parade, and she became a national celebrity. Below, a visitor at 1929's air show examines the Laird Swallow aircraft that Elder, a Ninety-Nine, placed fifth in during that year's Women's Air Derby from Santa Monica to Cleveland. (Right, Library of Congress; below, CAHS.)

When Charles Lindbergh—the "Lone Eagle"—landed at Lunken Airport on August 6, 1927, he was greeted as a hero. "As the wheels of the plane touched down, a screaming crowd lurched forward, broke the police lines, and almost ran into the path of the still-moving plane," recalled the Federal Writers Project history in 1942. Thousands lined the streets as his motorcade drove through the city to Redland Field, then home of the Cincinnati Reds. The day before, Army recruiters had distributed hundreds of photographs of Lindbergh, pointing out that he received his training in the Army Air Service. Lindbergh stayed at the Sinton Hotel, where reporters interviewed him throughout the day. That evening, he was honored at a dinner attended by 1,200 people on the rooftop of the Gibson Hotel. Cincinnati was one of 75 cities that Lindbergh visited following his historic solo transatlantic crossing on May 20 and 21, 1927. Even in smaller cities, such as Hamilton, Ohio, thousands gathered to watch the passing Lindbergh perform air stunts and drop messages to city leaders. (CAHS.)

Lindbergh (right) poses with Howard M. Wilson (left) and Charles A. Hinsch Sr. immediately after landing at Lunken. Wilson and Hinsch represented the Cincinnati Chamber of Commerce, where Hinsch chaired the airmail committee. Lindbergh had flown airmail as a young pilot in a DH-4 and had also been a barnstormer and stunt pilot. After his historic flight, young airlines doubled their route miles, airmail use tripled, and passengers quadrupled. (HDC.)

Lindbergh prepares to address the crowd at Redland Field. He had asked to speak at a large, outdoor setting so as many children as possible could attend. He believed that the younger generation would be the future of aviation. A group of Boy Scouts dressed as Native Americans presented him with a ceremonial headdress of eagle feathers, which he gamely wore while news photographers and motion picture cameramen snapped pictures. (HDC.)

Amelia Earhart poses with Elmer Schmidt of Cincinnati Aircraft Service in 1935. Earhart's Cincinnati visits were usually front-page news as she promoted aviation or raised money for flights. Sometimes she was just another pilot having her plane serviced. Earhart was not necessarily the best aviatrix of her generation, but she was the most inspirational. "Animated, vivacious, interesting, . . . and womanly" was how the *Cincinnati Enquirer* described her in 1929. (HDC.)

Crowds inspect the *Spirit of St. Louis* in 1927. The main fuel tank was in the forward fuselage, so Lindbergh had to use a periscope to see. Ryan Aircraft gave Lindbergh a new plane after his Paris landing. He also received numerous honors, including the first peacetime Medal of Honor and the Distinguished Flying Cross. Other, more unusual offers included a $5 million movie deal and a live monkey. (HDC.)

Jacqueline "Jackie" Cochran confers with Hugh Watson prior to a WLW interview at the Netherland Plaza in 1940. Cochran, who helped found the American cosmetics industry in the 1930s, became an outstanding air racer. Her achievements included being president of the Ninety-Nines and winning the 1938 Bendix Transcontinental Race. In 1937, she became the first woman to make an instrument-only landing. She won the Harmon International Trophy for outstanding woman pilot numerous times. As World War II began, Cochran advocated that women pilots be used for noncombat flights to free up male flyers. She studied how England utilized women pilots and became the first woman to ferry a bomber across the Atlantic. In 1942, Cochran began running the program that led to the Women's Airforce Service Pilots (WASP). In August 1943, the WASP merged with the Women's Auxiliary Ferrying Squadron (WAFS). Cochran remained head of the new combined branch. Pilot Nancy Love, who had headed the WAFS, was named head of the Ferrying Division command, which was moved to Cincinnati in June 1943. (HDC)

Cincinnati philanthropist Dolly Cohen pins a corsage on Eleanor Roosevelt, widow of Franklin D. Roosevelt, the 32nd president of the United States. Mrs. Roosevelt had just departed from an American Airlines flight at Lunken Airport around 1960. (Jack Klumpe Collection, University of Cincinnati.)

Paul Tibbets is seen attending the 2003 Lunken Air Show. As an Air Corps colonel, Tibbets flew *Enola Gay*, a B-29 Superfortress, on the first atomic bomb mission, which hastened the end of World War II. Earlier in the war, a design flaw caused B-29 engines to catch fire before takeoff. To show pilots how to take off safely, Tibbets successfully trained two WASPs to handle a B-29 named *Lady Bird*, then trained the male flyers. (CAHS.)

Cincinnati radio personality Jerry Thomas is one of 2,500 pilots that Don Fairbanks has taught to fly. Thomas is best known as a longtime WKRC disc jockey. Fairbanks and his wife, Pat, started Cardinal Air at Lunken in 1957. Fairbanks was inducted into the National Association of Flight Instructors Hall of Fame for his achievements as an instructor. (Don Fairbanks.)

Oscar Robertson cradles two trophies as he descends from an American Airlines plane at Lunken. The "Big O" played in two Final Fours and helped the University of Cincinnati Bearcats to two national championships in 1961 and 1962. He was the NCAA's first three-time basketball All-American. Robertson played for the Cincinnati Royals and is a member of the Pro Basketball Hall of Fame. (Jack Klumpe Collection, University of Cincinnati.)

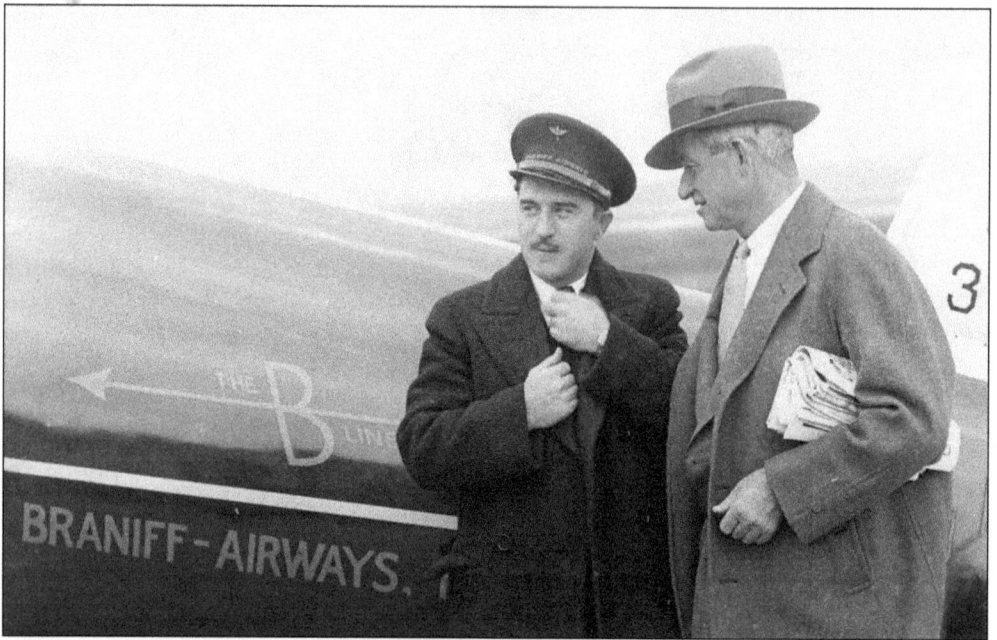

Will Rogers (right) and Braniff pilot Stanley T. Stanton share a lighter moment around 1930 at Lunken. The Braniff Airways Lockheed Vega was diverted to Lunken after being unable to land at its intended destination. Rogers was a humorist, vaudeville performer, radio personality, and movie actor known for his political and folksy commentary. He and pilot Wiley Post perished in a 1935 plane crash over Point Barrow, Alaska. (CAHS.)

John F. Kennedy speaks to a crowd at Lunken Airport on a 1960 campaign stop. State troopers and marching band members were in the crowd. Kennedy made multiple visits to the Queen City during his successful bid for the US presidency. Many high-profile people have chosen to arrive at Lunken rather than the Greater Cincinnati Airport to take advantage of Cincinnati police protection. (Jack Klumpe Collection, University of Cincinnati.)

The Beatles step down from their chartered plane at Lunken for their brief but boisterous August 27, 1964, concert at Cincinnati Gardens. Pictured are, from front to back, Paul McCartney, Ringo Starr, George Harrison, and John Lennon. While some frenzied teens waited at Greater Cincinnati Airport, the Fab Four landed instead at Lunken. "The 1,100 spectators let loose with a scream of delight which drowned out twin-engine aircrafts preparing to take off," reported the *Cincinnati Enquirer*. Forty-five reporters interviewed the Beatles briefly. About 50 teenagers swarmed the singers' cars and "for a few moments it appeared the singers' visit to Cincinnati might be spent at a Lunken Airport runway," the *Enquirer* noted. The Beatles did make it to the Gardens, where after two opening acts performed, they sang for 25 minutes. Steven Beasley, who was 10 years old at the time, remembers his parents taking him, his sister, and some friends to Lunken to catch a glimpse of the singers. He also recalls that Frisch's offered a set of Beatles drinking glasses that were popular with fans at the time. (Jack Klumpe Collection, University of Cincinnati.)

Pilot Douglas Corrigan helped build the *Spirit of St. Louis* yet was denied permission to attempt a nonstop transatlantic crossing himself. Nevertheless, Corrigan managed the feat in 1938 in a second-hand modified Curtiss Robin. He departed New York on July 17 en route to California, but ended up at Baldonnel Aerodrome, Ireland, on July 18, claiming cloud cover and a faulty compass took him off course. Now nicknamed "Wrong Way," Corrigan received a 14-day flying suspension, but was cheered during ticker tape parades in New York and Chicago. As part of a national tour, he visited Lunken in August. While crowds looked over his plane (below), Corrigan visited the Cincinnati Reds and hit a foul ball. He became a pop culture icon, referenced in everything from a Three Stooges' short to the Gobots franchise. (Above, Library of Congress; below, HDC.)

Five

Barnstormers, Daredevils, and Lady Birds

Hundreds gather to watch the conclusion of a Los Angeles–to–Cincinnati air race at Lunken in 1928. Precision aerobatics, parachutists, and flight demonstrations of battle tactics by Army and Navy bombers and fighters drew scores to Lunken Airfield as well as to Hugh Watson's Blue Ash Airport. Lunken soon became the hub for national air races, which were becoming all the rage. Concessionaires sold French-Bauer ice cream and ice-cold bottles of Vernor's ginger ale to the crowds. The proximity of the houses on the hill overlooking the airfield foretells the coming problems between homeowners and an increasingly busy airport. (HDC.)

Paul Davis (left) and Oliver Markland Walker prepare for a performance on July 7, 1926. Walker was on the barnstorming circuit for two years stunting and taking folks for rides in surplus World War I planes. Family life intervened, and eventually he went to work for Sun Oil. Walker died at age 96, having passed on to his family his memories of "air circuses." (HDC.)

Crowds head to the flight line at the 1929 Ford Reliability Good Will Tour at Lunken. Started by Henry Ford to win the public to aviation, the tour brought the premier pilots of the day to Cincinnati. The Metal Aircraft factory is shown in the background, with two Flamingos in front. Construction on Hangar 3 is seen in the foreground. (Morris Hall Collection, CAHS.)

Buddy Plunket (left) and Shirley "Whitey" Rauner prepare for a parachute exhibition at a Lunken air show around 1932. Billed as the Triangle Twins, the men were sponsored by Triangle Parachute, a company started by E.L. Hoffman at the old Globe-Wernicke Plant in Norwood. Rauner, well known regionally as a parachutist, won several awards and survived some rough landings. (HDC.)

An unidentified man poses with Jimmy Doolittle's famous Gee-Bee R1 Super Sportster at Lunken around 1932. Doolittle called the R1 the fastest, most dangerous plane he had flown at the time. Most pilots who had flown the craft had died or been seriously injured. Nevertheless, Doolittle won the Thompson Trophy Race with the Gee-Bee in 1932. Although he became internationally famous, he then retired from racing. (CAHS.)

This Breese monoplane, the *Aloha*, was one of only two planes to complete the deadly Dole Derby from Oakland, California, to Honolulu, Hawaii, in August 1927. Here, a Lunken ground crew turns the *Aloha* in preparation for the 1929 air show. The Dole race, sponsored by pineapple tycoon James D. Dole, was capitalizing on the excitement generated by Charles Lindbergh's solo transatlantic crossing in 1927. Dole offered a $35,000 purse, which attracted good pilots as well as several inept ones. Three flyers died while preparing for the race, two aircraft were disqualified, two crashed on takeoff, and two were forced to turn back. Of the remaining four planes that started, two disappeared over the Pacific Ocean. Calvin Coolidge ordered the Pacific Fleet to launch a massive air-sea search for the four missing crewmen to no avail. The *Aloha*, flown by barnstormer Martin Jensen, came in second. Art Goebel, a Hollywood stunt pilot, won the race in a Travel Air called *Woolaroc*. The real prize was just surviving the derby. (CAHS.)

An unidentified man leans out of the nose of a Keystone B-6A Panther assigned to the 11th Bomb Group at Lunken in 1932. Jiggs, of the *Maggie and Jiggs* comic strip, is pictured holding a bomb in this early example of nose art. The B-6A was developed for the Army Air Corps as a primary bomber between 1930 and 1934 then used for observation into the early 1940s. (HDC.)

The crowd watches in fascination as a crew fuels the American Airways Ford Tri-Motor at the 1932 air show. Seeing one of the big planes serviced was still a novelty to the non-flying public, many of whom had only driven automobiles for a short time. SOHIO, with its distinctive red-and-white logo, had a refinery in Latonia, Kentucky, providing a convenient fuel source for Lunken. (HDC.)

A Lunken ground crew surrounds a Ryan B-1 Brougham during the 1929 National Air Tour. Dogs, such as the one shown with the crew, were used to chase birds from the runway to avert bird-related accidents on takeoffs and landings. (Morris Hall Collection, CAHS.)

This Stinson R was the official pathfinder at the Cord Cup Derby in August 1932 at Lunken. Roy Hunt, an Oklahoma stunt flyer, won the grand sweepstakes in the transcontinental derby that year. Jiggs Huffman won the junior sweepstakes. Industrialist Errett L. Cord became famous for the Auburn, Cord, and Duesenberg automobiles but also ran Stinson Aircraft and the Lycoming engine company. He was also a founder of American Airways. (HDC.)

Two Wacos of the Linco Skywriting Company fly above Lunken at the 1933 air show. The top plane is the Waco Taperwing ATO, and the bottom plane is the Travel Air Model 4000. Taperwings were adapted for the Wright Whirlwind, radial engines and the wings were tapered similarly to those of military planes. These features made them ideal for stunt flying. Skywriting was a new concept and a novel advertising gimmick. (HDC.)

Resembling gigantic dragonflies, autogiro planes manufactured by the Kellett Company were used as observation planes during World War II. Here, an autogiro is displayed at Lunken in May 1933. On an autogiro, air flows up through the blades, and with a helicopter, air flows down. Autogiros never became widely used because they were prone to accidents. (HDC.)

Pictured in the above c. 1935 photograph is Lawrence Maxwell "Max" Schmidlapp, a well-known air racer as well as a Lunken businessman. A Princeton University alumnus and Hyde Park resident, he began flying in 1924. He won a Miami–Key West–Havana air race in 1937 after placing second in 1936. Schmidlapp cofounded the Wedekind-Schmidlapp Flying Service at the Parks Watson Airport in Blue Ash in 1931. He is most associated with Lunken, where he helped found the Queen City Flying Service, which operated out of Hangar 3. He was president of Queen City until ill health forced him to retire in 1962. During World War II, he was a transport pilot for the Army Air Corps Ferry Command. Below, he pilots his Aeronca C3 seaplane on the Ohio River around 1934. (Both, HDC.)

Alford J. "Al" Williams (shown here around 1940) pitched two seasons for a New York Giants farm team before becoming a naval aviator. He won the 1923 Pulitzer Trophy in a blue-and-gold Curtiss R2C-1. A tall, laconic Navy lieutenant, he set a speed record of 266 miles per hour a month later. His favorite racing uniform was a rumpled white shirt, tie, and blue trousers. He placed second in the 1925 Pulitzer. (HDC.)

Williams prepares to take off in his orange-and-blue Grumman Gulfhawk at a June 27, 1937, air show that was sponsored by the *Cincinnati Post*. Williams came "swooping out of the sky at 400 miles an hour," while describing his maneuvers on a penny-sized microphone attached to his throat, as radio stations WSAI, WCPO, and WLW broadcasted the show. (HDC.)

More than 75,000 people turned out for the dedication of Lunken's new terminal and administration offices, shown here on May 23, 1938. Parked in the right foreground is a bomber that became known as the B-17. The dedication had been delayed for a year because of a devastating flood in January 1937 that resulted in the sobriquet "Sunken Lunken." The Art Deco terminal, designed by Kruckmeyer and Strong, is still a Cincinnati landmark. The mural-sized paintings by William Harry Gothard inside the lobby are considered important examples of his work. Both the terminal and the paintings were funded partially by federal programs designed to raise the country out of the Great Depression. A restored B-17G named *Liberty Belle* was scheduled to appear at Lunken in late June 2011. However, the plane was destroyed on June 13, 2011, shortly after taking off from the Aurora Municipal Airport in Illinois. It was forced to make an emergency landing in a cornfield in Oswego, Illinois. All seven people on board escaped before the plane was consumed by fire. (HDC.)

People still dressed in their best clothes in 1935 to attend demonstrations of stunt pilots and parachutists on Sunday afternoons at Lunken. Some parachutists had "batwing" apparatus that enabled them to soar most of the way before opening their parachutes close to the ground. The crowds ate this up. None of the people in this photograph are identified. (HDC.)

Businessmen look over a Sikorsky plane in this undated photograph. The craft could be modified into a seaplane by replacing the wheels with pontoons. Igor Sikorsky designed the first four-engine airplane in 1913 in his native Russia. As transocean flights increased, he began specializing in seaplanes. By 1940, Sikorsky was an American citizen, and he began making the first helicopters that would be commercially manufactured. (HDC.)

Edmund P. Lunken poses with his Mustang racer, nicknamed "Buttonpuss" for his first wife, Dorothy, in this undated photograph. A serious racer, Lunken placed third in the 1947 Bendix. Airport businessman Elmer Schmidt always claimed Lunken's plane was sabotaged that year, preventing him from winning. Famed Hollywood stunt pilot Paul Mantz won the 1947 race as well as the 1948 Bendix, where Lunken placed fourth. (CAHS.)

This twin-engine Lockheed P-38 Lightning was exhibited at the 2003 Lunken Air Show. The P-38's high speed, performance at high altitude, and superior rate of climb made the Japanese fear it more than any other American fighter. The Lightning's capability for long-range flight made it highly desired in the Pacific, where distances were vast and mostly over water. (Charlie Pyles.)

Women pilots, or "lady birds," have been popular draws at Lunken air shows since the days of Amelia Earhart. Here, Helen Williams of Sabina, Ohio, prepares to take off in her Brunner-Winkle Bird at the August 1951 air show. Williams autographed the picture for Hans Dam, a pilot and aviation historian whose foresight resulted in many of the photographs in this book. (HDC.)

The shark-mouthed Curtiss P-40 Warhawk fighter (foreground) is the type Edmund P. Lunken flew in World War II. The plane is best known for service with the Flying Tigers in Burma and China. Behind the Warhawk are the Navy's F4U Corsair fighter-bomber and a F6F Hellcat fighter, which were instrumental in the defeat of Japan. The Planes of Fame Air Museum of Chino, California, loaned the planes to Lunken in 2003. (Charlie Pyles.)

This replica of Orville and Wilbur Wright's Flyer at the 2003 Lunken Air Show is a reminder of Ohio's aeronautical heritage that inspired Cincinnatians to embrace aviation. On December 17, 1903, Orville made the first manned aircraft flight at Kitty Hawk: the Flyer became airborne under its own power, flew forward at a steady speed, and landed on ground no lower than the ground the flight started from. (CAHS.)

One repeat performer at Lunken that never fails to draw crowds is *Fifi*, the only World War II B-29 that is still flying, shown here on June 12, 2011. The *Enola Gay*, famous for dropping the first atomic bomb on Hiroshima, was a B-29. *Fifi* was produced late in the war and never saw combat. B-29s carried an 11-man crew had a 20,000-pound bomb capacity and a 3,500-mile range. (Bob Johnson.)

Caro Bayley Bosca smiles for the crowd at the 1952 air show from the cockpit of her Pitts Special, "the love of my life . . . small, black, and sleek." She was the Women's International Aerobatics Champion in 1951. That same year, the Federation Aeronautique Internationale of France awarded her the Bleriot Medal, presented annually to record setters in speed, altitude, or distance categories. The Springfield, Ohio, woman received tuition for flying lessons as a graduation present. She worked at Patterson Field (now Wright Patterson Air Force Base) to earn money for advanced lessons and more flying time. As a WASP, Bosca was stationed at Biggs Field in El Paso, Texas, flying missions to test antiaircraft capabilities and ground radar. B-25s and B-26s were two of the many military planes she flew. After the WASP was deactivated, Bosca taught flying in Florida, barnstormed across the South with an aerobatics troupe, and began competing in aerobatics events. She and her husband, Orsino Bosca, raised four children in Springfield. In 1988, she was inducted into the Ohio Aviation Hall of Fame. (HDC.)

This C-54, called the *Spirit of Freedom*, was used in the Berlin Airlift. CAHS member David Brightwell piloted the plane in 2011. The plane, loaned by the Berlin Airlift Historical Society, was featured at several Lunken air shows from 2000 to 2005. (Charlie Pyles.)

Henri Mignet designed the Flying Flea small enough to fit inside a home garage. Ed Nermier built this Flea for industrialist Powel Crosley in 1935, the year it won a prize at the Miami Air Maneuvers. The plane was almost destroyed in a major fire that swept Crosley's hangar in 1937. The plane's parts were stored in a barn until 1956, when they were uncovered, restored, and reassembled. (CAHS.)

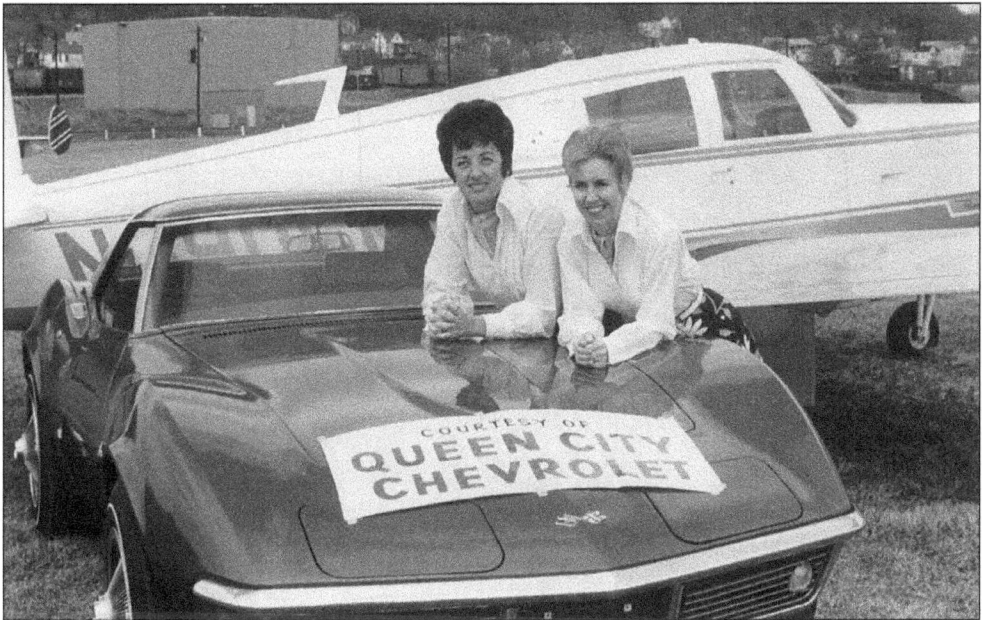

Pat Fairbanks (right) of Cardinal Air Transport and Training and friend Mary Ann Halmi relax at Lunken in 1969 after participating in the Powder Puff Derby. Fairbanks, a flying instructor, once checked out Neil Armstrong in a Mooney plane that he wanted to fly. She flew in many derbies over the years. Originally the Women's Air Derby, humorist Will Rogers coined the name "Powder Puff" in 1929. (Don Fairbanks.)

Teresa Stokes performs her wing-walking routine at the 2003 air show, while Gene Soucy flies the plane. Stokes and Soucy are more than air show performers; Stokes donated one of her kidneys to Soucy. Wing-walking was one of the most hazardous and popular acts of the early air circuses. Even Charles Lindbergh performed wing walking during his barnstorming days. (CAHS.)

Don Fairbanks of Cardinal Air flies his Knight Twister in a race. Fairbanks began racing in 1971. At the second race of his career in Cape May, New Jersey, he witnessed a tragic accident where four pilots died. Fairbanks continued to enjoy racing for years, eventually setting four speed records and competing in the International Air Races in Mexico. (Don Fairbanks.)

The pilot of this Navy Grumman F8F Bearcat talks with visitors at the 1978 Lunken Aerospace Show sponsored by General Electric. A modified F8F set a speed record for piston aircraft at 528 miles per hour in 1989. Its ancestor, the F6F Hellcat, along with more aircraft carriers, created mobile airfields in the Pacific that gave the Americans the edge in the air from mid-1942 on. (General Electric Aviation.)

Navy SEAL parachutists (above)—probably the Chuting Stars—assemble prior to donning jump gear at the 1978 air show. In the background are the Air Force Thunderbirds T-33 jets, featured later in the show. Below, a SEAL descends, steering his paraglider. SEALs are trained for the most difficult and deadly missions where a waterborne approach is needed, where extreme stealth is required, and where small groups must work in isolated conditions without reinforcement, such as the 2011 mission to kill al-Qaeda leader Osama bin Laden. With frogmen roots in World War II underwater demolition teams, SEAL candidates undergo rigorous, unrelenting training in many combat scenarios, with only a small percentage of candidates becoming bona fide SEALs and being awarded the distinctive gold Special Warfare Trident, featuring an anchor and an eagle clutching a trident and flintlock pistol. (Both, General Electric Aviation.)

Tom Griffin, previously of Cincinnati, navigated an earlier model of this B-25J Mitchell with the Doolittle Raiders in April 1942. The unexpected raid proved US bombers could reach the distant islands of Japan, and it was a morale boost for Americans following Pearl Harbor. Paul Redlich and Phil Rountree of the Tri-State Warbird Museum flew the *Axis Nightmare* to Lunken for a June 2011 appearance. (Bob Johnson.)

On February 20, 1963, in a previous incarnation, the B-25J *Wild Cargo* made a dramatic belly landing at Lunken with jammed landing gear, one engine dead, and the other failing. The pilot walked away, and his copilot bailed out safely. Firemen rescued trussed alligators and crates of snakes and turtles that were headed for the Cincinnati Zoo. Since then, *Wild Cargo* has been restored; it's one of 17 B-25s flying today. (Greg Morehead.)

Six

FLOODS, FOG, AND MISHAPS

Morris Hall, photographed driving the truck, prepares to tow a wrecked Monocoupe back to Lunken Airfield from Canton, Ohio, in August 1929. The boys and young men in coveralls doubtlessly talked about the wreck and salvage for weeks afterwards and probably volunteered to help Hall ready the plane for the trip back. Elmer Schmidt once told *Cincinnati Post* columnist Si Cornell that Embry-Riddle's flyers had so many forced landings in the early days that Higbee Embry purchased a flock of carrier pigeons to help locate the downed pilots. The idea was that a pigeon would travel on each flight so in case of an accident, the pilot could attach a message to one of the bird's legs. However, the plan was never implemented. (Morris Hall Collection, CAHS.)

Johnny Johnson grins sheepishly after a close call in his Waco 10 on October 22, 1928, at Lunken. He ground looped the plane and wound up with wheels pointing skyward. In a ground loop, the plane turns suddenly and violently. This usually happens during taxiing, takeoff, or landing. Johnson's formal attire was typical for performing flyers of that time. (Morris Hall Collection, CAHS.)

A group of unidentified folks pose in front of a Waco 10 that cracked up at Lunken in 1929. The plane, part of the Embry-Riddle fleet, was piloted by Stanley C. "Jiggs" Huffman at the time of the accident. Notice the large landing lights at the base of the struts, above the lower wings. The lights were used for night landings before the advent of runway lights. (Morris Hall Collection, CAHS.)

Spectators admire R.A. Hosler's G&G Special racer at Lunken in August 1930. The plane was outfitted with unique single-wheel landing gear, which was designed to prevent wingtip damage. Unfortunately, Hosler's plane crashed during a racing accident that day. (Morris Hall Collection, CAHS.)

Spectators look over the wreckage of an American Airlines DC-3 bound for New York that cracked like an egg when it skidded into a high water dike at Lunken around 1938. The pilot was about to touch down when a strong gust of wind blew the plane to the left of the landing strip. Three of the 11 people on board were hospitalized. AA estimated damages at $60,000. (HDC.)

Okey and Martha Bevins wait while their Waco 9 is fueled at Lunken in this undated photograph. They were well-known local pilots. They met at Lunken when then Martha Croninger was one of the first women student pilots and Okey was her instructor. He was also an airmail pilot for Embry-Riddle. They married in 1929. Shortly after, Okey attempted a nonstop transcontinental solo flight. He departed from Los Angeles but only made it to Willard, New Mexico. Okey then went to work for Aeronautical Corporation (Aeronca Manufacturers) at Lunken. By 1935, the couple moved to Wilson, North Carolina, where he was a flight instructor. He flew back into Lunken that October and headed for Detroit. Sadly, the pilot, with 16 years' experience, did not make his destination. On October 18, Okey took off from Lunken. He encountered treetop-level fog as he neared Mason, Ohio. At approximately 10:31 a.m., his plane hit the 831-foot-tall WLW radio antenna tower and spun in. The *Cincinnati Times-Star* reported that Bevins was killed instantly. (Okey Bevins Collection, CAHS.)

Okey Bevins's crash into the WLW radio tower made front-page news in Greater Cincinnati. Like today, people were drawn to the scene of the tragedy. The impact hurled his plane into a straw stack at an adjacent farm. Investigators speculated that Bevins's plane might have brushed a guy wire supporting the tower. The plane struck the tower at about 600 feet; the tower was not damaged. (HDC.)

Six people died when this Ford Tri-Motor crashed into the bank of the Little Miami River just after taking off from Lunken on August 8, 1931. Pilot M.T. Odell lost control of the Embry-Riddle plane when the starboard propeller broke off, causing the subsequent loss of the motor. The plane somersaulted before smashing to earth. This was the first fatal accident in American Airways' Embry-Riddle division. (HDC.)

Bystanders rubberneck at a Taylorcraft seaplane that plunged into the Ohio River on September 3, 1941. Pilot Lonny Thompson of Seaplane Fliers, Inc., and a student were thought to be flying out of Lunken that day when their plane struck a guy wire on a Cincinnati Southern Railroad bridge that the men were flying under. They were uninjured and were picked up by the *Greenbrier*, a dredge boat. (HDC.)

Auto tycoon Harry J. Tucker's Lockheed Vega 5, named the *Yankee Doodle*, was photographed at Lunken in the autumn of 1928, shortly before a crash that claimed the lives of Tucker and pilot Charles B.D. Collyer. Collyer set a transcontinental speed record of 24 hours and 51 minutes in the Vega on October 24, 1928. They were returning to New York on November 5 when they crashed in Arizona. (Morris Hall Collection, CAHS.)

Maj. William A. Cahill of the 359th Air Corps Reserve Observation Squadron parachuted out of his disabled Boeing P-12, landing safely on the Kentucky shore of the Ohio River on November 29, 1940. The plane was at 4,000 feet when the Bond Hill resident jumped. It crashed about six miles east of Coney Island. (HDC.)

Build an airfield at the juncture of the Little Miami and Ohio Rivers, and the water will come. Water surrounds a partially constructed hangar in March 1929, foreshadowing more costly flooding. After this flood, city council planned to spend $145,000 to build a levee ranging from 18 to 25 feet high. A pumping system was also to be installed to handle water that underground tiles could not drain. (CAHS.)

The January 1937 flood caused $32 million in damage in Greater Cincinnati and crested at 79.99 feet at Lunken. Three hangar rooftops and the top of the new terminal are visible in the photograph. Twelve square miles were covered, and the airport was closed for 17 days. Amazingly, only one person in Greater Cincinnati died in the flood. (Morris Hall Collection, CAHS.)

Water surrounds the terminal and debris lies in the road in the aftermath of the April 1948 flood. The brick-and-steel wall of the Cincinnati Aircraft Service building collapsed at the west end and the roof partially collapsed. The damage at that building totaled $10,000. Waters reached a maximum of 20 feet at Lunken, where a total of 22 buildings were flooded. (HDC.)

Seven

FAMOUS AND FORGOTTEN PLANES

Two Embry-Riddle employees look over the flight line at Lunken in October 1928. By the late 1920s, E-R's fleet included Wacos, Fairchilds, Monocoupes, and Ryans. Almost all aspects of aviation had changed since World War I; these planes and E-R's operations reflected that. Aircraft design became more aerodynamic, and engines were more reliable. Basic instruments included altimeter and tachometer, while oil pressure and fuel gauges became more standard. Seat belts and parachutes were found in more and more cockpits. Standardized flight instruction courses, such as those offered by E-R's flight school, became more prevalent. (Morris Hall Collection, CAHS.)

Thomas Hiner, a flying weatherman, stands in front of a Curtiss 0-1 Falcon biplane at the Army Air Corps (AAC) hangar in 1935. The Falcon was designed as an observation plane for the Army Air Service in World War I. While still covered with fabric, it had a unique aluminum fuselage with steel bracing. The functional two-seater never saw combat. Only 279 Falcons were manufactured; by 1935, the craft was obsolete. (HDC.)

John "Millie" Milholland, an Embry-Riddle employee, poses in 1928 with a Ryan M-1, similar to the *Spirit of St. Louis*. When Lindbergh asked T. Claude Ryan to build him a plane, Ryan said he could build it for $6,000, minus the instruments and the engine. The result was a special plane called the "NYP" (New York–to–Paris) powered by a Wright Whirlwind J-5C radial engine. (Morris Hall Collection, CAHS.)

Important flyers and planes inevitably visited Lunken following historic flights. Here, the Fokker *Josephine Ford* used by Navy lieutenant commander Richard E. Byrd on his 1926 North Pole flight attracts visitors at Lunken later that year. That May, Byrd and pilot Floyd Bennett departed from and landed at Spitzbergen, Norway. It was later discovered that they had not reached their destination. Byrd shifted his attention to the South Pole, and on November 28, 1929, he and his three-man crew flew over the South Pole in a Ford Tri-Motor with skis. He was promoted to rear admiral for this achievement. Later, as a civilian, Byrd flew many Antarctic expeditions. His plane, shown here, is the first F-VII Fokker built. Rheinhold Platz, Anthony Fokker's chief designer, became famous for designing German fighters during World War I, including the widely regarded Fokker D.VII and the Dr.1 tri-plane flown by 80-kill ace Manfred von Richthofen (the "Red Baron"). After the war, Fokker began building planes for the US Army and US Navy. The company was called the Netherlands Aircraft Manufacturing Company for a time to disassociate the planes from World War I. (HDC.)

Laura Ingalls, pictured at left standing on a sawhorse, received the Harmon Trophy for her flying achievements in 1934. She made the longest solo flight—17,000 miles—by a woman pilot. Ingalls left from New York on February 28 and flew first to Mexico and then to Chile. She crossed the Andes Mountains to Rio de Janeiro, then to Cuba, and returned to New York on April 25. She became the first person to make a solo flight by land plane around South America. Later that year, she had the fastest plane in the Liberty Treasure Hunt at Lunken. Her Lockheed Air Express Special is seen below at Lunken. In 1936, she placed second behind Louise Thaden in the Bendix. (Left, Library of Congress; below, HDC.)

Morris Hall (above, far right), who held several jobs at Lunken in the 1920s, poses with his unidentified crew before a Sikorsky S-38A in October 1928. Sometimes referred to as "The Explorer's Air Yacht," the nine-seater S-38 was the first Sikorsky amphibious plane produced on a large scale. Private pilots, airlines, and the US Navy and Army Air Corps used these planes. Sikorsky enthusiasts included Charles Lindbergh and Howard Hughes. Filmmakers Martin and Osa Johnson flew a zebra-striped S-38 and a giraffe-patterned S-39 to travel throughout Africa, creating films and books about the African continent. Sikorsky amphibians set several records, including altitude and speed with specific loads. (Both, Morris Hall Collection, CAHS.)

Edmund P. Lunken owned this Beech Staggerwing. Louise Thaden and copilot and navigator Blanche Noyes—both Ninety-Nines—won the Bendix in a C-17R Staggerwing in 1936, the first year that women competed with men. It was called the Staggerwing because its lower wing was positioned forward of the upper wing to improve visibility. Its retractable landing gear was rare at the time on private planes. (CAHS.)

This c. 1932 photograph shows James R. Wedell standing with the Wedell-Williams 44 (as in a .44 bullet) racer in which he won the 1933 Thompson Trophy. He and Harry Williams created the plane for Wedell, but other racers began buying the planes and beating him. The Wedell-Williams racers dominated the Bendix and Thompson races between 1931 and 1935. Wedell died in a June 1934 crash caused by a student pilot. (CAHS.)

This 1929 eight-passenger Flamingo sold for $23,800, a considerable price at the time. Jimmy Angel flew a similar Flamingo named El Rio Caroni to Venezuela in 1937 to search for gold. In 2011, Karen Angel, the explorer's niece, was still trying to persuade Venezuelan authorities to release the rare plane so it could be preserved. (William T. Larkins, CAHS.)

Arthur Bussy came in second in the 1939 Bendix Trophy Race in this one-of-a-kind Bellanca Tri-Motor monoplane, seen here at Lunken that year. Sicilian immigrant Giuseppe Mario Bellanca designed the Bellancas. He was a consultant at the Wright Aeronautical Corporation in the 1920s and started the Columbia Aircraft Company in 1927, building high-wing monoplanes. Later that year, he formed Bellanca Aircraft Corporation. (CAHS.)

Actor Wallace Beery's Bellanca Skyrocket prepares to take off at Lunken around 1936. Beery, who appeared in 250 movies and won a Best Actor Oscar in 1931, was reputed to be a hard-drinking, sometimes violent man. His other plane, appropriately, was a Howard DGA-11. Legend has it the Howard was nicknamed DGA ("Damned Good Airplane") by a bootlegger who was impressed by the craft's capacity for hauling liquor. (HDC.)

A Stinson Lycoming Model A in American Airline's fleet is serviced at Lunken on February 16, 1937. The plane was a striking blue with orange trim. AA began using the tri-motor in 1935. It carried eight passengers on regional flights. (HDC.)

This Aeronca K was one of the last Aeroncas developed at Lunken before the company moved 30 miles north to Middletown, Ohio. The original K was a disappointing craft, so the manufacturer developed the twin-engined KC Scout. The Aeronca Chief was the next step, and it proved much more successful. (CAHS.)

A Stout Tri-motor taxies at Lunken around 1930. Henry Ford acquired the Stout Metal Airplane Company in August 1925. This Ford 4-AT-B was an 11-passenger commercial airliner. The Navy and the Army used the "Tin Goose" for transport. In 1942, the plane shown above crashed in Billings, Montana, killing the pilot and copilot. (CAHS.)

Airmen of the 359th Air Corps Reserve muster in front of a Douglas 0-46A around 1940. The Douglas was a two-seat observation plane with a Browning .30-caliber machine gun mounted in the front, plus one that could be aimed by the observer-gunner in the rear. The star on the underside of the wing shows that this is a pre–World War II plane. (CAHS.)

A crewman services a Gee Bee Model X Sportster for a race around 1930. Lowell Bayles flew the Model X to second place in the 1930 All-American Air Derby. He streaked to first in the 1931 Thompson Trophy in a black-and-yellow Gee Bee Z Super Sportster, winning $7,500 (five years' wages for the average worker). He died in a fiery accident in the Z just months later. (CAHS.)

Blue Horizons Travel Club operated this Douglas DC-7C to exotic destinations in the late 1960s through early 1970s. Lunken's terminal is at the far left. The DC-7Cs started flying transcontinental flights in 1956 for Pan American Airlines and also made international flights. The plane could carry up to 105 passengers comfortably, because it had a longer fuselage. (Bob Garrard, CAHS.)

Cadet Pvt. Nick Nimersheim smiles from the cockpit of his Army Air Corps P-12F at Lunken in 1940. By the onset of World War II, the obsolete planes were used as radio-controlled targets to train pilots and gunners. Astute moviegoers will recognize the P-12 as the type of plane that attacked King Kong on the Empire State Building in 1933. (HDC.)

A Lockheed C-141 Starlifter, called the "Hanoi Taxi," leaves on its final visit to Lunken on September 12, 2003. The first Starlifter flight was on December 17, 1963, the 60th anniversary of the Wright brothers' first powered flight. During the Vietnam War, the planes transported men and cargo back and forth from Vietnam almost daily. It was designed to carry up to 154 troops anywhere around the globe. (Charlie Pyles.)

This Douglas C-47A, the military version of the DC-3, sits on a special dolly that permits it to move sideways into the Proctor & Gamble hangar at Lunken in May 1971. The C-47, affectionately referred to as "Gooney Bird," was widely used as a transport in every theater of World War II. Postwar, many of them were converted into commercial transports for smaller airlines. (Bob Garrard, CAHS.)

Eight

LIFE AT LUNKEN

Martha Bevins flashes her dimples from the cockpit of her Waco 9 around 1935. In a time when flying was still a man's domain, women had to prove themselves, but once they did, they were accepted. After her husband Okey's horrific death in a 1935 plane accident, Martha continued to fly. As World War II progressed, she trained with the fourth class of the WFTD at Midland, Texas. When WFTD became part of the WASP, Martha flew aircraft out of Romulus Air Force Base in Michigan. After the war, she remarried and lived in Erlanger, Kentucky. (Okey Bevins Collection, CAHS.)

Embry-Riddle Company issued this bright orange flyer in 1928 to promote its services. CAM-24 on the Flamingo's tail refers to E-R's airmail contract, which it won from the US Post Office at a bid of $1.47 per pound of mail. Pilots flew the mail daily from Cincinnati to Chicago via Indianapolis. It was a dangerous job. To keep the contract, they had to deliver the mail daily, despite heavy fog and rough weather, using only visual landmarks on the ground to guide them. They began flying passengers on the airmail route in 1928. A Waco was used if only one or two passengers accompanied the mail. If more passengers had to be flown, a Ryan B-1 was used, according to Stephen G. Craft of ERAU. (CAHS.)

This c. 1935 photograph shows Lunken employees and passengers clustered in front of a Ryan Brougham similar to the one used to ferry passengers on E-R's airmail routes. The only person identified in this photograph is Martha Bevins (kneeling, far left). The Bevinses' lives were so intertwined with flying that they spent part of their honeymoon in 1929 flying a Lockheed Vega around, advertising *True Story Magazine*. (Okey Bevins Collection, CAHS.)

The Little Miami River snakes along Lunken Airport in this c. 1960 photograph. Beechmont Avenue is shown in the foreground. In 1925, John Dixon "Dixie" Davis and Wendell Pavey started the Dixie Davis Flying Field in the area above Beechmont, just south of the area then referred to as Union Levee. (CAHS.)

Airmail pilots often roomed together because it was cheaper. This c. 1929 photograph shows a group wearing the practical clothing needed for flying in cold weather in open cockpits, including wool sweaters, knit caps, and knee-high boots. The only person identified is Millie Milholland (back row, far right). In 1929, E-R pilots flew 79,751 pounds of mail and 692 passengers. (CAHS.)

Paul Riddle flies a biplane over Cincinnati's Withrow High School in December 1926. It's not known who took the picture. Aerial photography became extremely popular in the early days of flying. Most companies operating at Lunken offered the service. Farmers were a frequent target. The aerial photographer would snap a number of farms, develop the film, then drive from farm to farm showing off the photographs and taking orders. (ERAU.)

Cincinnatian Gordon Mougey Jr. poses for a publicity photograph at Lunken in 1935. A popular attraction at air shows, he flew a Travel Air Speedwing for skywriting. In 1934, he won the Kroger Trophy for Rhythm Acrobatics, plus numerous other cups and cash prizes in the mid-1930s. He flew the new Laird monoplane at the June 1937 *Cincinnati Post* air show, performing skywriting and aerial stunts. (HDC.)

This Waco plane, once owned by the Lunken family, appears to be part of the YKC series of cabin tours built in 1936. The Weaver Aircraft Company began building open-cockpit planes in 1919 and was producing a variety of closed-cabin planes by 1930. The company went out of business in 1947, when the anticipated postwar aviation boom failed to develop. (Lunken Family Collection, CAHS.)

Cincinnati postmaster A.L. Behymer stands on a Waco 10 to muster support for a $500,000 bond issue to expand Lunken as a municipal airport in 1927. Voters approved the issue and work began to make the airfield one of the largest and busiest in the nation. Blaine Johnson of Johnson Flying Service owned the plane, named *Master Walter*. (HDC.)

Charles Lindbergh mailed a letter in this envelope to Master Walter Johnson for his birthday in 1928. The boy was a relative of Blaine Johnson of Johnson Flying Service. Lindbergh, who flew the mail early in his career, took it up again briefly in 1928 to promote use of airmail. The 10¢ stamp features the *Spirit of St. Louis*. (HDC.)

This c. 1929 photograph shows Embry-Riddle pilots escaping boredom between flights with a friendly game of craps. They didn't have a lot of down time. In 1928, the pilots flew 35,665 miles between Cincinnati and Chicago, carrying 35,667 pounds of mail, 2,014 pounds of express cargo, and 270 passengers. (Morris Hall Collection, CAHS.)

Pilots and mechanics in a light-hearted moment engage in a snowball fight during the bitterly cold winter of 1929. Pilots had to contend with 0 to -5 degree weather, which caused iced wings, potentially hazardous runways, low visibility due to snow and fog, and bone-chilling conditions in open cockpits. (Morris Hall Collection, CAHS.)

In this c. 1936 photograph, three employees of Queen City Flying Service stand ready in pristine uniforms reminiscent of Texaco advertisements to serve the public. Charter flights, airplane services, and sales of Waco planes were some of the services offered at Hangar 3. The planes are Waco YKS-7s. (HDC.) .

Melville Schmidt (left), his brother Elmer Schmidt, and their wives (unidentified) relax in front of a Waco 10 at Boyers Field in Ross, Kentucky, on September 3, 1931. The brothers started refurbishing crashed planes and selling them to pilots at Boyers. In 1935, they rented Hangar 2 at Lunken and started their Cincinnati Aircraft Service, where they met many noteworthy pilots, including Amelia Earhart, and trained pilots for World War II. (CAHS.).

Looking like the well-dressed man of the air for 1930, Larry Hazelton holds a blown cylinder head from his plane. Although details of the incident are not known, the outcome could have been fatal if it happened while Hazelton was aloft. It is likely that the cylinder blew while he was taking off or landing. While Hazelton escaped unharmed, hundreds of pilots each year were killed or severely injured in accidents caused by equipment malfunctions, inclement weather, and pilot errors. The season appears to be winter. Hazelton is wearing heavy leather winter coveralls with a shearling collar, insulated boots, and leather gloves designed for some flexibility despite the cold of an open cockpit. He is wearing a bowtie underneath and probably a pair of itchy wool long johns. (CAHS.)

The Lunken crash truck, loaded with the remnants of a plane, pulls up in front of a hangar around 1928. Operated by the Embry-Riddle Company, this truck salvaged plane wrecks. (ERAU.)

Lunken's original terminal was built with funds from the 1927 bond issue. In this c. 1930 photograph, the sign that says "Passenger terminal for all Airlines" refers to Embry-Riddle and Mason & Dixon flight services. It appears that airport management was preparing to construct a parking lot at the time. Within seven years, ground was broken on an impressive new brick terminal. (CAHS.)

Well-dressed passengers wearing boaters prepare to board a Mason & Dixon Flamingo in 1930. Most of the early air passengers were men flying on business. Air travel was still fairly turbulent at the time. Vibrations from the engines caused passengers' bones to ache during longer flights, and airsickness was a real problem. Stewardesses had to be registered nurses to deal with any physical problems that passengers experienced. (CAHS.)

Visitors stream to already-crowded bleachers at Lunken's 1930 dedication. Crowds jammed into the airfield to watch the military and stunt flyers. One attraction was the introduction of the slot-winged Doodle Bug, an experimental plane made by air racer J.S. McDonnell. The plane could remain stable in any position, take off in 100 feet, accelerate rapidly, and execute a dead-stick landing in less than 40 feet. (CAHS.)

Frank Hawks and his wife, Edith, pose at Lunken around 1930. He worked in Hollywood as a stunt pilot but was more famous for flying point-to-point races and setting numerous aviation records. The first Northrop Gamma, built in 1932, went to Hawks and became the *Texaco Sky Chief*. He set several records in the plane, including a nonstop flight from Los Angeles to New York in 13 hours and 27 minutes in June 1933, averaging 181 miles per hour. In 1936, Howard Hughes rocketed the same course in 9 hours 27 minutes, beating Roscoe Turner's old record by 36 minutes. Hughes flew a Gamma called the *H-1 Flying Bullet* that he leased from Jackie Cochran and had modified by his own mechanics. Hawks cancelled his planned record attempt after Hughes's achievement. Hawks starred in a long-running radio serial called *Hawk's Trail*, on the silver screen in *Klondike* in 1932, and in the serial *The Mysterious Pilot* in 1937. He died in 1938 when the Gwinn Aircar he was flying with a prospective buyer apparently hit a power line and crashed. (CAHS.)

Charles A. "Bunnie" Hinsch Jr. (left), Joy Hodges, and Max Schmidlapp pose in front of a Waco EQC-6 around 1940. Hodges, a stage and movie actress, may have been in Cincinnati for a performance. She signed a five-year contract with RKO Pictures in 1935. In 1937, she starred on Broadway with George M. Cohan in the musical *I'd Rather Be Right*. That was also the year she advised radio announcer Ronald Reagan to get rid of his glasses if he wanted to make it as an actor and introduced him to her agent. Hinsch and Schmidlapp were well known in their own right at Lunken. Hinsch and his sister paid for Lunken's first radio control tower, which attracted more airlines. Schmidlapp was co-owner of Queen City Flying Service, which sold Wacos at Lunken. He was also a trophy-winning racer. (HDC.)

This c. 1928 photograph shows Hangar 1 under construction. It was the first of three buff-brick-and-steel hangars completed by 1930. The original terminal is to the right. It was the first civilian hangar at the airfield; the old Army Air Service hangars were moved earlier from Grisard Field. Hangar 1 was the headquarters for Embry-Riddle's operations and later for American Airlines. (CAHS.)

Bas-relief stylized airplanes adorn the side of Hangar 1, the most decorative of the three brick hangars. Lunken adopted the stylized plane as part of its logo. The hangars were designed by Kruckmeyer and Strong and built by the Warm Brothers Company. The hangars and new terminal were part of a large WPA-Cincinnati project that included outdoor recreation facilities, including a playground, golf course, and tennis courts. (CAHS.)

Mechanics ready Al Williams's Gulfhawk prior to his performance at the air show while visitors watch on July 27, 1937. Audiences loved to watch Williams fly too fast in a series of orange, white, and blue Gulfhawks sponsored by Gulf Oil. He became aviation manager at Gulf after leaving the Navy in 1930. Williams advocated for increased US air power, eventually leaving the Marine Corps Reserve over his outspokenness. (HDC.)

In this c. 1929 photograph, a cross-section of automobiles is seen parked in front of Hangar 3 as it is constructed. Middle-class folks who were fortunate enough to own an automobile frequently chose Ford Model As, Plymouths, Pontiacs, and Buicks, while wealthier people drove Packards and Duesenbergs. All three hangars were completed by 1930, when Lunken was dedicated as a municipal airport. (CAHS.)

Five friends gather in front of a Curtiss-Wright Travel Air Sedan in 1937. The men are, from left to right, unidentified, Gene Kemp, Herb Cramer, Don Griggs, and pilot Dan Henry. Curtiss-Wright absorbed Travel Air prior to 1937 but continued making the popular Travel Air. (HDC.)

A cluster of elated pilots stands before Bunnie Hinsch's Luscombe Phantom with their trophies after an unknown air race at Lunken around 1939. Hinsch is third from the right. Other people identified are Max Schmidlapp (fourth from the right) and Dan Henry (far right). The Phantom was a powerful and demanding plane to fly, and Hinsch was expert at it. He was an investor in the Luscombe Airplane Corporation. (HDC.)

This aerial view shows the layout of the newly renovated airport, with the Air Cab Service hangar to the left. In addition to the stunting Aeroncas and Al Williams's performance in his Gulfhawk and bombing a mock fort, visitors enjoyed Gordon Mougey's aerobatics and skywriting in a Laird monoplane. Wendell Flemming executed a dead-stick landing in a Taylor Craft. For such a landing, the pilot typically cut the engine at 5,000 feet, gliding in to land as close as possible to a specific mark. A total of 75,000 to 100,000 people were estimated to have seen the flying from various locations around the city, with 50,000 of those at the airfield to meet the celebrity flyers, to look over new planes on display, and to be entertained by the aerobatics. There was an emphasis on youth, with the *Cincinnati Post* presenting the air show as a tribute to the Junior Aviators Squadron, an organization sponsored by the newspaper. Aviation students from the Automotive High School helped with parking and giving directions. (HDC.)

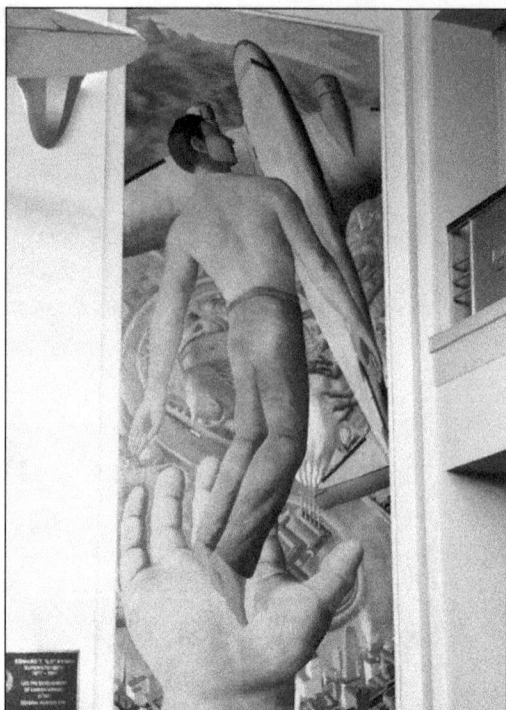

Flying not only freed people's bodies from gravity's hold, it also freed their dreams and aspirations. Artist William Henry Gothard's 1937 oil-on-canvas murals in the terminal lobby symbolize the concept. One mural shows man yoked in place before flight. The mural above shows man freed of gravity's restraints, ascending from the hand that previously constrained him. The man rises, along with an airplane, over Cincinnati. The billowing smokestacks of factories below illustrate industry keeping pace with aviation. The murals were already installed in the terminal when the 1937 flood occurred. They were quickly removed and stored off-site. They were in place for the official dedication of the airport's improvements in May 1938. Gothard won a WPA contest to paint the murals. He later became chief conservationist of the Cincinnati Art Museum. (Dick Swaim.)

John W. Pattison, son of Ohio governor John M. Pattison, prepares for a trip in his two-seater *Jean D'Arc* during his unsuccessful campaign for Congress in 1936. Pattison, who was vice president of Central Life Insurance Company, was an original investor in the Lunken Airport Company. He served as a captain in the Army Air Corps Reserve. Later, he was director of the National Air Transport Company and American Airlines. (HDC.)

Dorothy and Edmund Pattison (E.P.) Lunken share a happy moment at Lunken in 1948. During World War II, E.P. served with the Sixth Air Force, tasked with guarding the Panama Canal. He served first as a reconnaissance pilot and later as a fighter pilot, flying a P-40 Warhawk and P-38 Lightning. He and Dorothy had two sons, Edmund Backus Lunken and Eshelby Frederick Lunken II. (Lunken Family Collection, CAHS.)

Lunken manager George Frodge poses with a Piper Aztec around 1957. When Frodge supervised airport operations in the 1950s, Lunken was no longer a hub for commercial passenger airliners. Greater Cincinnati Airport (CVG) had taken over that task. Lunken remained busy as an airport for private pilots and a reliever airport for CVG. Improvements made in the 1960s drew small commuter services and corporate aircraft. (Frodge Family Collection, CAHS.)

This F-86H Sabre was most recently flown by the Washington, DC, Air Guard. It languished on the Lunken Playground for years before being moved to the airport in 1999. This type of fighter, built by North American Aviation of Columbus, Ohio, saw service during the Korean War. Jackie Cochran became the first woman—under Chuck Yeager's tutelage—to break the sound barrier in a similar Sabre in 1953. (Charlie Pyles.)

Don Fairbanks leans against an Aeronca TAL-65 after soloing at Lunken on August 17, 1944. He had been taking flying lessons with Harold Cook while home on leave after completing 30 missions with the Army Air Corps. Fairbanks was a gunner and flight engineer on B-24s with the Eighth Air Force out of England. His crew flew classified missions for the Office of Strategic Services (OSS), the forerunner of the CIA. OSS dropped supplies to various resistance groups and dropped agents who sabotaged German equipment and supplies, as well as operatives who helped direct the underground and carried vital information to the Allied Command. Fairbanks was awarded the Distinguished Flying Cross, the Air Medal with three Oak Leaf Clusters, and the Presidential Unit Citation. In 1945, he became crew chief on a B-25 for the Air Transport Command (ATC), operating out of Lunken. After a tour in Japan, Fairbanks was discharged in 1955 as a master sergeant. He and his wife, Pat, operated Cardinal Air at Lunken from 1957 until the early 1990s, when they moved to Clermont County Airport in Ohio. (Don Fairbanks.)

Hal Shevers teaches a ground school course for student pilots in 1963. Shevers may be best known as the founder of Sporty's Pilot Shop, which began at Lunken in 1961, but he is also recognized as a flight instructor. He pioneered the first three-day ground school courses in 1963. He and the late Al Passell, a fellow instructor, were inducted into the National Association of Flight Instructors Hall of Fame. (Hal Shevers.)

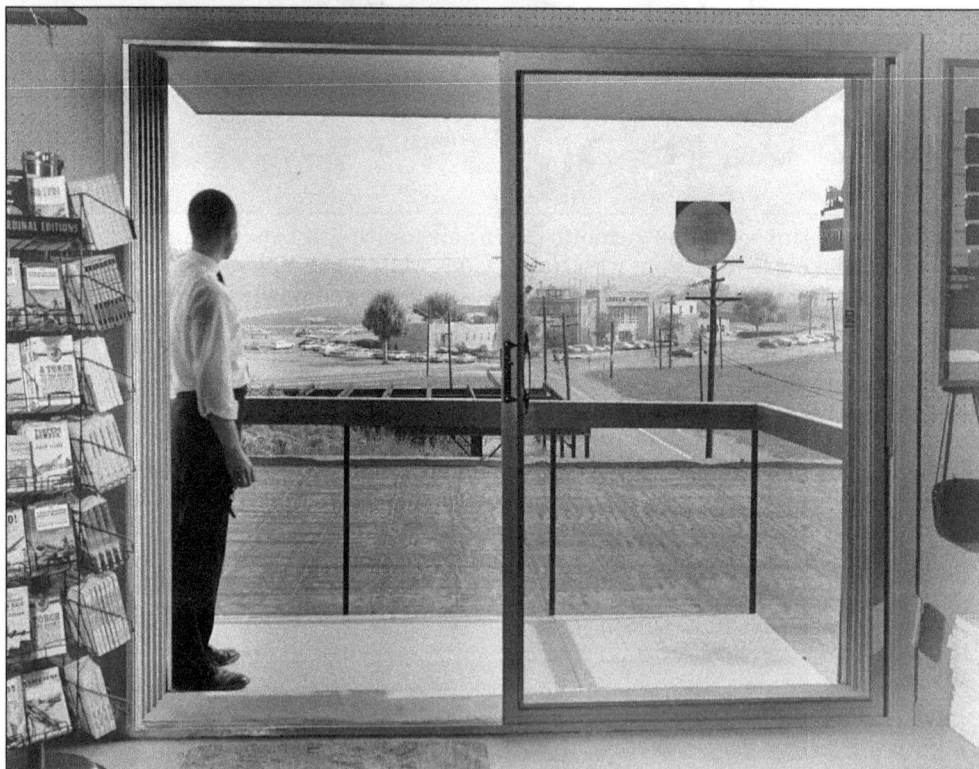

In this c. 1965 photograph, a man stands inside Sporty's Pilot Shop at Lunken looking out onto the terminal. Today an aviation merchandising mogul, Hal Shevers began selling radios by mail, using the trunk of his car as a warehouse. He operated Sporty's at Lunken from 1961 until 1971, when he moved to the Clermont County Airport. Shevers's ventures today include the Sportsman's Market and Sporty's Academy. (Hal Shevers.)

Hal and Sandy Shevers stand in front of a Piper Aztec around 1972. Of his 10,000 flying hours, 2,000 have been in Aztecs. The Sporty's Foundation, which was started to encourage aviation education, donated $30,000 in 2010 for University of Cincinnati aviation scholarships and $19,200 to the Boy Scouts of America. An Eagle Scout himself, Shevers was awarded the Boy Scouts' Distinguished Eagle for aviation achievements. (Hal Shevers.)

Pat Fairbanks smiles after finishing her helicopter flight test in June 1978 in a Bell 47G at Lunken. She became the first woman radio station helicopter pilot in greater Cincinnati, flying with WCKY announcer Ted Florko over the city for rush hour traffic reports. She later earned her helicopter flight instructor license. Pat and her husband, Don, sold helicopters at Cardinal Air and also trained people to fly them. (Don Fairbanks.)

The two trainers shown here have strong connections to Lunken. Frank Mayo Fairchild, the airport's first control tower operator, developed an important air traffic control course around 1940. Prospective aviation cadets took Mayo's course during World War II, as did students in the Civilian Pilot Training program. Later, the cadets took primary training in Stearman PT-17 Kaydets, such as the one above, photographed by Diane Redlich in 2007 at the Tri-state Warbird Museum at nearby Clermont County Airport. Pilots took advanced training on craft such as the Navy SNJ, shown below, photographed by Bob Johnson at the 2011 Lunken Aviation Days. The SNJ, flown by Todd Winemiller in 2011, was the Navy's version of the trainer; the Army's designation was the AT-6 Texan. Both trainers were identical and were built by North American Aviation of Columbus, Ohio. (Above, Diane Redlich; below, Bob Johnson.)

With the periodic whoosh of a propane flame as the only sound, a hot air balloon ride is an unearthly, tranquil experience, as riders gradually drift higher until the world below looks like a H.O. gauge railroad setting. Above, a crew readies a balloon for a dusk ascension at the 1978 air show. A Parisian made the first manned balloon flight in late 1783. Some balloons used hot air and others used hydrogen. During the Civil War, the Union army used tethered balloons to observe Confederate activity and positions. Balloons were also used for observations during both world wars. Most Americans, however, became aware of balloons as entertainment spectacles as far back as the 1880s. By the beginning of the 20th century, balloon rides and exhibitions were popular attractions at county fairs. Today, one of the largest balloon festivals is held at Taos, New Mexico. In Ohio, the Middletown Balloon Festival draws thousands of visitors annually. (General Electric Aviation.)

A B-17G, the *Aluminum Overcast*, drops in to pay a visit, attracting aviation fans to Lunken in 2011. This type of bomber had four 1200-horsepower air-cooled radial engines with General Electric B-22 turbo-superchargers. It carried 13 M-2 .50-caliber Browning machine guns, a normal bomb load of 4,000 pounds, and a crew of 10. The *Overcast's* engines were made by Wright Aeronautical in Evendale, now General Electric Aviation. (Bob Johnson.)

This red-and-white DC-3 was used to discharge skydivers over Kings Island near Mason, Ohio. They jumped shortly before dusk at the evening performance, using the fountain near the main entrance as a reference point for their jumps. At the 1978 Aerospace Show, its wings provide shade for visitors. (General Electric Aviation.)

Lynda Kilbourne of Newport, Kentucky, stands beside her 1946 L-17 Navion named *Bazooka Baby Armed and Dangerous*. On September 10, 2011, she flew the missing man position in the Missing Man Formation during the Lunken Aviation Days weekend to commemorate the terrorist attacks on September 11, 2001. Kilbourn, a member of the Ninety-Nines, learned to fly to honor her late father, who was a World War II P-51 fighter pilot. (Bob Johnson.)

The Cincinnati Aviation Heritage Society's office inside Lunken's terminal displays many mementos and images of aviation in southwestern Ohio over the decades. A radio-controlled J-3 Cub hangs from the ceiling. To the right is the original rotating beacon from the airport in Falmouth, Kentucky. CAHS is seeking memorabilia while working to expand its museum and research library. (Charlie Pyles.)

"Golden lads and girls all must, as chimney-sweepers, come to dust," wrote Shakespeare in *Cymbeline*. Ruth Rowland Nichols (above) embodies that sentiment. "The Flying Debutante" was a Wellesley graduate and a Ninety-Nine who met Powel Crosley Jr. at Lunken in October 1930. She persuaded him to sponsor her attempt to be the first woman to fly across the Atlantic. Crosley loaned her a crimson-and-cream Lockheed Vega, which she named *Akita*, a Dakota word meaning to discover or explore. Nichols set a women's altitude record of 28,743 feet in the Vega on March 6, 1931. That June, she made her Atlantic attempt but was forced to stop after a landing mishap sidelined her with several broken vertebrae. She returned to flying, but by the end of 1932, she and Crosley parted ways. Nichols moved from front-page headlines to page-four briefs, but her endeavors inspired a new generation of flyers. That's true of pioneers in any field, and certainly of many of the people discussed here. They are gone, but their legacy continues. (Cyclopedia of Aviation Biography Collection, WSU.)

INDEX

Visit us at
arcadiapublishing.com

www.ingramcontent.com/pod-product-compliance
Lightning Source LLC
Chambersburg PA
CBHW050651110426
42813CB00007B/1980